The Bounty Writer

Andrew Don has been a journalist for nearly 40 years—30 of them operating as an independent. Andrew has written extensively for the national press and business-to-business magazines—print and online—and he has been a news editor, features editor, deputy editor, launch editor and editorial consultant. The Bounty Writer, published by Beachy Books in 2021, is his third book. His first, Fathers Feel Too, a book about miscarriage and stillbirth, was published by SANDS in 2005. Virtuality, a self-published ebook, followed in 2011. He lives in West Wales with his wife, Liz, a Rhodesian Ridgeback and a DuCorps Cockatoo. He has two adult children. His passions are wildlife, long-distance walking, literature and music.

The Bounty Writer

How to Earn Six Figures as an Independent Freelance Journalist

Andrew Don

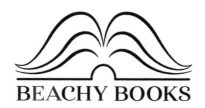

BEACHY BOOKS

First published by
Beachy Books in 2021
(an imprint of Beachy Books Limited)
www.beachybooks.com

1

A CIP catalogue record for this book is available from the
British Library.

ISBN: 9781999728366

Set in Adobe Caslon Pro

For Jim Muttram with thanks for all the advice and encouragement, Stephen Clackson, for helping me get my foot in the door and Val Clarke, without whom I would never have got my Pre-entry Journalism certificate and gone on to enjoy a wonderful career.

Contents

Chapter 1

Fear, hunger and angles

'I learned that courage was not the absence of fear, but the triumph over it. The brave man is not he who does not feel afraid, but he who conquers that fear'

Nelson Mandela

I did not need to be a household name to earn six figures as an independent journalist. Nor did I need an 'ology' with letters after my name.

All I needed was an overwhelming fear of destitution, a hunger for news and an instinct for seeing an angle in, ostensibly, even the most mundane. For I learned that nothing is mundane when approached with originality.

A modicum of skill proved helpful during my career as did my propensity to rage against naysayers. Anyone who said 'no' to me got the equivalent of *'I'm Henry the VIII I am'* in a loop, Patrick Swayze-style.

Luck, too, played an essential role, the relationships I cultivated and timing.

I have a genetic disposition to crippling anxiety and depression, which 'nurture' exacerbated. Frankly, my achievement of nine 'O' levels shortly after Mum died of cancer was nothing short of miraculous.

Mum's cancer played a major role in discombobulating and unbalancing me as did her propensity in my early childhood to play good-cop-bad-cop. She suffered extreme mood swings so that I never knew where I was with her from one minute to the next.

I broke down in the first months of sixth form and took a year off pursuing odd jobs in London. These included cleaning out animal poo in Palmer's Pet Shop in Camden Town, photocopying *World in Action* scripts on a massive Xerox copier at Grenada TV, in Golden Square, Piccadilly, and stuffing envelopes and packing books at a taxation book publisher near Green Park.

The next academic year, I attended a mediocre sixth-form college, which did nothing for nurturing my potential. Nor did my addiction to Valium, which had been prescribed from my mid-teens after initially pilfering them from my dad's second wife who had bottles of the tranquiliser in their bedroom cupboard. I performed woefully in my 'A' levels with a Grade E in my best subject, English, let down by one specific paper, which I stared at for three hours writing nothing but my name.

That I scraped through with what was deemed a by-the-skin-of-your-teeth pass in those days must have meant I achieved top marks, or as near as damn it in the other papers. I performed slightly better at Law where I scrambled a C—a joke because I excelled at English and Law had been a desperate afterthought.

I had originally signed up at college to do the three sciences but realised, within the first few weeks, I was completely out of my depth. I had some notion I was going to be a farmer. Don't ask! I didn't know who I was and where I was going. Dad wrote a letter to the college explaining that I had suffered 'emotional' issues since the death of my mum, and I was allowed to change courses. Students were normally required to do three subjects but, in the circumstance, the college reluctantly agreed that I would do two.

My mental health made any further education out of the question despite an interview at Salford University which offered me a conditional place.

I also suffered from deafness, which I hid for as long as possible from as many people as possible, masking it with a talent for lip-reading, constantly 'popping' my ears when listening, and reading body language.

I was hardly set for journalism super-stardom in the mould of Piers Morgan or Andrew Neil. God's gift to journalism, I most definitely was not. My shorthand was atrocious despite achieving 100 words per minute for exam purposes—a feat I never measured up to again. I would concentrate so much on hearing that I would tense and get cramps in my hand, which made fluid shorthand a challenge.

Somehow, I managed to scribble accurately what people said, although I struggled to read it back. A future editor and mentor, Jim Muttram, read my shorthand better than I, a remarkable decoding feat I marvel at to this day.

I survived nearly 40 years on shorthand that mixed Teeline with my own dodgy shortenings, but thankfully I have been aided more recently by technology.

What I lacked in terms of ear-hand coordination, I more than made up for with a pit bull terrier personality: give me a bone and I would rip your arm off before I would let you take it from me—the most important qualification, together with a good memory, I advocate, if you are going to earn big money as a freelance or independent.

If I can do it, with my baggage and hang-ups, then why not you?

Independent journalism is not particularly glamorous or romantic in most cases and it can sometimes be mundane. The press events and parties I frequently attended as a staff journalist were not financially viable once I was self-employed: rubbing shoulders with people as different from each other as Sir Douglas Hurd and the late Paula Yates did not pay the bills once I was compensated by the word, the magazine issue, or the day, rather than drawing a monthly payslip plus expenses.

I was chained to my desk, but I could have lunch with Liz, my wife, whom I married three years into my career independence. She is a self-employed travel agent and worked from our home from around the turn of the millennium. Typing away with my dog sleeping at my feet and a parrot on my shoulder beat working in Quadrant House in Sutton, Surrey, where I had last worked as an employee as deputy editor of *SuperMarketing*.

I earned more over the totality of my career and for years at a time than I ever imagined. The decision to become self-employed was one of the best I have made. I attribute my success to the right mentors who had my back, perfect timing and my own tenacity and determination to succeed despite both mental and physical issues.

For me, my news hunger is instinctual, like breathing. You are either a natural news reporter or you are not. The hunger for news cannot be taught. The technical skills can. Technical skills without hunger will not bring long-term success or sustain the independent journalist when times are hard.

Chapter 2

The pot of gold at the end of the rainbow

'The best way to predict the future is to create it'

Abraham Lincoln

I transformed my life in October 2019, aged 57, after 35 years in full-time journalism—the last 30 of them self-employed.

I saved into a pension throughout my career, boosting it during my peak-earning years between 1998 and 2010, because I knew there had to be an endgame. I knew the energy I had aged 28, when I went self-employed, would not be the same into my half-centenary and that I would need to plan for getting older.

So many people do not plan for escaping the rat race because they think the opportunity to do so is unimaginably far away. The last trimester of life creeps up soon enough and you find yourself wondering, like your grandparents before you, where all the time went—and pruning roses.

Turning 57 was my fulfilment of a dream. I moved with Liz, dog Saphira and parrot Rocky, from north London to a tiny village in West Wales, two minutes' walk from the beach and the coastal path.

I am living my dream, sitting in my library at an antique bureau, on which sits my laptop and a decanter of single malt.

I never thought a better work-life balance would have been possible when I began my career as a trainee reporter at the *Fleet Street News Agency* in Exmouth Market, in the City of London, in 1984. John Rodgers, who owned the agency, hired me thanks to the recommendation of one of my mentors, Stephen Clackson—then assistant editor of the *Sunday Express Magazine*—and a subsequent interview.

Rodgers' news editor, the late Jim Wardlaw, who was on holiday at the time of my interview, seemed to take an immediate dislike to me when I started work. He took me for a pint after work on his first day back to size me up and I must have said something to get his back up to the extent there was no way back. I sometimes compensated for my lack of self-esteem by acting overconfident and I do not think it went down well with my new boss.

Wardlaw would tell me to stick my head up a dead bear's bum many times a day. He did, to be fair, tell *everyone* to stick their head up a dead bear's bum. With others it was largely in jest, and I think people took it in good humour as it was generally meant. When he said it to me, with a sneer, it was clear to me that he would have liked nothing more than for me to disappear somewhere where the sun never shone.

He sat me down in the office a few months into the job, in earshot of colleagues, and told me I would never make it as a journalist and to give it up. He sought to destroy my fragile confidence by feigning a paternal concern for me. He told me how he did not want to see me become one of the so many Fleet Street journalists he knew who carried on in the job year after year but were not any good. He really did not want that for me, he said. I remember the sick feeling in the pit of my stomach as he said that and the way the room spun.

The more he feigned concern the angrier I got. I was not going to let a man I regarded as a bully stop me following this path that I had chosen or, that had chosen me. I was determined to be brilliant at my job, to work like a demon, to prove doubters wrong and to make decent money.

I was desperate to succeed in journalism. There was nothing else I could do. I remember walking from Farringdon Station to Exmouth Market in those early days and gazing up at one of the windows in *The Guardian* building and telling myself I would write for the newspaper one day. I am not sure that I really believed I ever would. I have had many features published in *The Guardian* and *The Observer* since going into business for myself.

I had fought worse than Jim Wardlaw to get to where I was in my life—on the brink of a career that would see me find happiness and success.

Industry bible *Press Gazette* reported in February 2017 that one in three freelance journalists was on state benefits and typically earned £20,000 a year. I earned more than five times that for a good part of my freelance career. Somehow, I made a rare financial success of independence.

Good independent journalists should earn good money. Most struggle in my experience, which is why I decided to write this book. If I had to give one explanation for my earning power, it would be one word: 'desperation'. I had to succeed. There was no other option.

Perhaps I did so well because I entered my teenage life and adulthood at rock bottom. I could either give up or fight for a life. I chose to fight for a life—a good life. It was that fight that made me successful as did my determination to never feel so isolated again.

Self-employment is not for everyone. You cannot give in to distraction—it is not an opportunity to enjoy more leisure time but probably to have less free time. Working from home means you never switch off. It is difficult to separate the two environments because you will be mostly working from your home unless you are one of those independent journalists that goes into other people's offices.

You have the benefit of not having the commute. I had a two-hour journey each way when I worked for *SuperMarketing* between 1986 and 1990. I would get into work for 8am before everyone else. I was getting up at 5am and leaving home at 6am. Rolling out of bed and starting work without travelling on crowded, smelly trains was a novelty that still feels wonderful 30 years later.

An independent journalist must work obsessively to earn more than their employed colleagues. It can be lonely. I would not recommend it if you do not have a partner with whom you share your life or a loving family nearby. I had none of those when I became self-employed and I spent the first few years feeling utterly isolated until I met Liz.

I underwent extensive counselling to come to terms with childhood demons during my first years of self-employment. Working alone, with no one to talk to apart from work contacts on the phone, was soul-destroying. I would spend day after day in my own company. I saw friends at the weekend, but when I came home my only company was my dog and, at that time, a timid budgie called Vincent van Gogh. That was a mouthful, and it was no wonder he could not repeat his name. I teetered on the edge of mental illness, but I had fire in my belly, and I kept hope alive.

Journalists are, by and large, highly principled, apart from a few who would sell grandpa to slave traders if it meant getting a by-lined scoop. We are, for the most part, people who want to right injustices, expose corruption and, in business-to-business, help readers to run their businesses better and expose those who try to scam them.

Some of us have an overinflated view of our own importance but, as a group, journalists in the UK are integral to free speech and democracy.

Hard work and long hours, a rigorous work ethic, a character able to rise beyond rejection and survive knockbacks are just a few basic requirements to keep the money rolling in.

You are on the right track if you are a first-rate communicator, you scrutinise every bit of information presented to you or that you uncover, you have an insatiable appetite for asking the questions no one else asks and you have a healthy disrespect for the public relations industry, and those people and organisations that hide behind it.

A competitive spirit is essential. I had to write a better article, whatever I wrote and whoever I wrote for, than those who were covering the same story on other publications.

I ensured I got facts and figures 'rivals' did not get, or angles and stories they missed or the significance of which they failed to grasp. I also deemed it a priority that, where a story was announced as part of a sophisticated corporate communications strategy, I appeared in print with it before anyone else.

I did not, of course, succeed with this 100% of the time or even 90% of the time, but it is what drove me, apart from the desire to earn a good living. My competitive spirit kept me hungry and motivated. I never lost sight of the fact that independent journalism was a business as well as a vocation.

Staff journalists need not pay regard to the commercial aspects of the publications they write for—or, at least, they should not have to. Advertising revenue and who advertises should not be their concern. This can prove tricky for small editorial teams on weekly and monthly Business to Business (B2B) publications where it is not unheard of for management and sales teams to exert influence on which companies to include in editorial coverage.

I have certainly experienced this but, as far as I was concerned, my job was always to get damn good stories and I did not care a jot about the commercial aspects, even if it affected the security of my own employment.

Most independents do not have the luxury of being able to research a story for days on end if they have bills to pay. Sometimes you might have to write advertorials or B2B features that the publication you are writing for regards as 'ad-gets'. Never turn that sort of work down. Work is work.

My priority was to keep the money coming in and generate a blend of work—the proper bona fide journalism as well as the softer stuff. Think of it like having a balanced pension portfolio. It contains a mix of investments so that when one type of asset falls another type of asset increases in value.

Successful independence requires a balancing act between your highest aspirations and eating. It is as much about character as it is about talent.

Do not believe all the nonsense you are told when training to be a journalist about the need to be thick-skinned. A thick skin helps survive rejections, but sensitivity and empathy are more important if you are going to get your interview subjects to open up to you, editors and section heads to commission you and accountants to pay you promptly.

Intelligence and inquisitiveness are more important than academic qualifications. Some of the best journalists I know are neurotic, angst-riddled individuals—not thick-skinned hacks who care more about their egos than the veracity of the story they are pursuing.

I am thin-skinned. I am also an angry man, although I am far more mellow since moving to Wales than I used to be, aided by a beautiful landscape and lots of sheep. Liars and those who are, to put it more kindly, economical with the truth make me angry and those who use public relations (PR) to distort the truth and get in the way of the story.

Politicians and civil servants who do not answer the question or deal in half-truths infuriate me. You may recall prime minister Boris Johnson's special adviser Dominic Cummings' Donald Trump-style arrogance and rudeness to an *ITV News* reporter just doing his job on Brexit night.

'Are you going to walk along asking inane questions? Is that your best move?' he spat. Many of us winced watching the footage. There could be no possible excuse for behaviour like that short of his cat getting run over and we, as journalists, must always hold such people to account and never let them bully and intimidate.

Anger at people like Cummings has been key to my success. The angrier I am, the more dogged I am in getting the story, getting people to talk to me and getting past gatekeepers so I reach the horse's mouth.

But your subject must believe you are going to be fair with them. What a journalist thinks of as fair might not live up to their subject's scrutiny. More good stories that are truly based in fact are nailed because interviewees trust the journalist or, at least, as far as anyone ever trusts journalists.

I frequently found myself explaining to B2B interviewees that I was not a tabloid journalist and that we were on the same side.

'Can I see what you are going to write about me before it goes to press?' they would ask. It was not company policy, I told them. No journalist worth their salt would ever show what they were writing before it went to press. My paymaster was the publication that had commissioned me. I was not their paid PR executive.

'However, I do promise you I will be scrupulously fair and that I uphold the highest journalistic integrity,' I concluded.

Nine times out of ten that worked. You just must stand your ground—firmly and politely. They might put the phone down but anyone who aspires to be anybody in their career will have the intelligence to realise that pissing journalists off is not a good idea. Treat people right and you will reap what you sow.

As Jim Muttram repeatedly instilled in me, you must always be fair. Fairness may still make someone look bad in print, but that will be when they have made themselves look bad by their own behaviour or utterance. Former US president Bill Clinton's insistence he did not 'have sexual relations with that woman' is a good example.

Criticism of Donald Trump was fair because of the power of his influence. Such people should be held to account and that is what a free press achieves. Journalists do not have to be peddlers of 'fake' news. All they have to do is report what comes out of Trump's mouth. His declaration that opening the US economy in time for Easter 2020 was 'a beautiful timeline' when COVID-19 was still raging is a case in point, even more so that just weeks earlier on February 26, he largely dismissed the risk to the American people.

Likewise, Trump's ridiculing of a disabled journalist deserves calling out. Such a person demeans his office in my opinion and in most right-thinking people's opinion.

Ultimately, you get the best out of people when they warm to you. Watch back the best of the old Sir Michael Parkinson interviews. Why does he get people to touch on sensitive areas of their life? He makes them feel safe. He gently leads them in a paternal way to where he wants them to go.

You need trust, co-operation and good links with other journalists and contacts. Word soon gets around both customers and interviewees if you cannot be trusted, especially in specialist B2B journalism where you will frequently have to speak to the same people many, many times about many, many different stories.

A successful independent should not hide behind smoke and mirrors. You want to make yourself the first port of call for publications that want a reliable journalist—not second or third choice. Do not grumble, do what is asked of you and more, always return calls, emails, social media callouts and texts immediately if you can or as soon as reasonably practical. Effuse enthusiasm. Everyone likes to hire someone who shows excitement about an assignment even if it is about bakery oven widgets or telematics for fleet owners. I have been there and done that.

Editors and section heads like to hire other journalists who love their job, turn in a great bit of writing and submit it to deadline.

Not everyone gets the opportunity to interview the biggest A-listers and may not even want to. You should tackle every assignment with gusto. This is easier said than done. Life can get in the way, but if you are not enthusiastic about every piece you research, it will show in your writing.

In brief

- What is your endgame? Where do you want to be in 30-40 years? Plan for it today. Review and adjust your plan periodically to meet your changing desires, commitments and circumstances.

- Do not give others power over your sense of self-worth and self-belief.

- Turn 'negative' emotions, such as anger, into positives that further your agenda.

- Work like a demon.

- Maintain social/family contacts.

- Show a competitive spirit.

- Network, network, network.

- Show enthusiasm even if you do not feel it. The feeling will come.

- Treat every assignment like it's the big one—love what you do and let others see that you love what you do.

Chapter 3

The best education is a practical one

'Don't let school interfere with your education'

Mark Twain

I did not always want to be a journalist, although I loved writing from the time I could hold a pen. I was penalised at school, however, because of my illegible handwriting. My primary school was big on pupils using cumbersome italic pens. My exercise book looked like a landing pad for sick blue seagulls. Every time I was graded in handwriting tests, I got an E. I argued it should not matter that my handwriting was illegible because the content was great. My teachers said it did not matter how good the content if no one could read it. Idiots, I thought. Surely pencil and ballpoint pen would have sufficed or a typewriter.

My childhood dream was to become a veterinary surgeon, a pop star or a veterinary surgeon who had a few hit records—a bit like Noel Fitzpatrick, aka the Supervet, who, in the early days of his career, somehow managed to juggle veterinary surgery with acting, according to his book *Listening to the Animals: Becoming the Supervet* (Orion Publishing Co).

A dismal head for numbers—but not for trends and patterns—put paid to me getting anything beyond a CSE Grade 1 in maths, which had an 'O' level Grade C equivalency, and I was rubbish at anything practical including laboratory experiments.

I was the kid the chemistry teacher would not let anywhere near a Bunsen burner. When we had to dissect a mouse in 'Human' Biology I was sick, but I somehow got a Grade A at 'O' level in the subject proving you do not have to butcher furry little critters to know what you are talking about.

I was cack-handed: if I had to remove a spleen, I would probably have got rid of the pancreas and a testicle. This had become patently obvious in compulsory needlework in the first year of secondary school when kindly classmate Miriam took pity on me and would thread my needle after I stabbed myself numerous times.

None of this bode well for stitching up dogs post-op. I do, however, have a good singing voice—at least, I think I do—but success was limited to applause at Karaoke Crazy in Golders Green where I went by the alias of *The Man of a Thousand Names*.

But I did have a talent and that was an imagination that I was able to put to good use and put into written words to tell an inventive story—when the teachers had the patience to decipher my handwriting.

I doubt whether many children at school could have written a trilogy, *The Life Story of a Parker Pen*, and for their English teacher to comment 'I felt *frissons* of terror'. The thought of my wonderful English teacher, Clive Lawton, feeling *frissons* of terror was a disturbing one and I felt pangs of guilt. My writing was not well structured. It was the furthest thing from journalese possible, but I loved it.

Dad was manager of an office equipment shop that sold manual and electric typewriters from exceptionally cheap and cheerful Silver Reeds to outstanding office Adlers that were the Rolls Royce of typewriters. This is where I taught myself to type and spent hours in his shop doing so. I was a prolific poet for much of my early life and I wrote my first poetry on adding machine roll from dad's shop.

It should have been obvious what I would end up doing for a career. I think Mum's two biggest fears were that I might turn out to be gay, mediocre or both. I drew a moustache on a woman's face in a magazine once, and she was convinced I was homosexual, like it was akin to being a mass murderer. 'Promise me you'll never do that again,' she implored.

It was Mum, dying of cancer aged 44, who informed me I would never become a vet and that, with my ability to write, I should think about becoming a journalist. I was naive and I rarely watched the news. The earliest news bulletin I can remember was about Archbishop Makarios, who died just three days before Mum.

After Mum died, I went off the rails—drink, prescription drugs, attempted suicide. I got rejected by a Middlesex County Press trainee scheme after treating a role play of reporting on an accident on a construction site like an audition for *Gone with the Wind*.

I remember the news editor doing his best to stifle laughter. I was an utter plonker. It was a pity because I had got shortlisted based on my submission of an article about a family of Travellers who had camped on local Green Belt and opened up to me about their lives and struggles.

I enrolled in a writing correspondence course, which taught me how to write different types of pieces from short stories for women's magazines to film scripts and features. My correspondence course tutor was a man called Ken Ashton. There was a former National Union of Journalists (NUJ) general secretary of the same name, but I do not know if they were one and the same and it never seemed important enough to find out.

I got my first article published because of this course—in the *Jewish Chronicle*—a satirical self-effacing piece about an atypical Jewish teenager who dressed up in leathers and drove around Golders Green on his motorbike. It was headlined *The ton-up kid*. The fact I did not have a motorbike and could not afford leathers was neither here nor there. It was my ability to show my interviewees at the London College of Printing (LCP) that I had already been published and been paid for it that got me on the Pre-entry Journalism course there.

I emerged at the end of it with my certificate on the strength of my feature writing. I hated the layout and design part of the course, which I was rubbish at and which accounted for far too many of available marks, in my opinion.

I demonstrated at college I was good at getting great angles and I would bust a gut for an original story. I went on a couple of work placements including one at music weekly *Sounds* where the famous Garry Bushell worked at the time. The other was the *Harrow Observer*, a publication owned by Middlesex County Press, which had previously rejected me.

Neither of those placements opened any doors, but it was all good experience that gave me an insight into how the world of journalism operated. They gave me an early taste of my chosen career. I made myself useful and a few small articles I wrote appeared in *Sounds* and the *Harrow Observer* during the short time I worked for them.

I also got commissioned by magazines called *American in Britain* and *Educational Courses in America and Britain* after editor Russell Dean got in touch with the LCP. The call from Dean came during the holidays when I was doing a mindless job straightening prongs on components at a warehouse on the North Circular. Dean commissioned me a few features—my first proper freelance commissions. I promptly walked into the warehouse manager's office and said something to the effect of: 'I don't need to do mindless jobs like this anymore. I'm leaving.' And with that I marched out, head held high, and feeling as if I had just had an infusion of something illegal.

In brief

- If looking to change careers or start your career, have something to show editors—a piece you wrote for the local newspaper, a pop concert you reviewed.

- Do a correspondence course and go on a relevant college course.

- Seek work placements.

- Take every opportunity you can to contact editors.

- One commission could be all you need to prove to college or job interviewers that you have what it takes.

Chapter 4

Mentors are a journalist's best friend

'Blessed is the influence of one true, loving human soul on another'

George Eliot

I have always had mentors in my life—people I looked up to and who had a major influence on how my life turned out, from Clive Lawton, an exceptional English teacher at secondary school, to Stephen Clackson, who took me under his wing when I joined the LCP.

Clackson—who was to later become news editor of the *Evening Standard*—opened doors for me when he was assigned to me as part of my LCP training. Clackson reminded me of Mick Jagger—more rock'n'roll than em rules and overmatter. We took an instant liking to each other. He took his mentorship seriously and he was enormously encouraging at a time of my life when I needed my self-esteem plumped up.

He saw potential in me and I, in turn, trusted him—probably a first for me. Clackson helped me secure an interview at the *Fleet Street News Agency* because he knew the owner and recommended me. The wages were barely enough to pay my rent, food and train fares, but it was a foot in the door. I am grateful to agency owner John Rogers for the fact it started me on a career that has been my saviour. The *Fleet Street News Agency* taught me the art of selling a story—one that held me in good stead during my self-employed years—and an insight into how national newspapers operated.

I remember when Rogers telephoned to offer me a trainee position. I leapt in the air and whooped several times when I put the phone down. When people asked me what I did for a living, I could say I was a journalist. How cool was that! Me, a 'Gentleman of the Press'. This was a new start, a chance to make something of myself.

By the time I went solo, Clackson was working on the *Evening Standard* and I was able to sell him stories from time to time.

Jim Muttram, another mentor, had been newly promoted from news editor to deputy editor of weekly trade newspaper *SuperMarketing* when he interviewed me for the position of deputy features editor in 1986, which was my fourth staff job in journalism after I left Middlesex County Press, owner of the *Harrow Observer*. The local newspaper group had eventually hired me, albeit in the unsatisfying role as advertisement feature writer. While it was not the best career move, I got to eat in a lot of restaurants and wrote about them afterwards. The only rule was I could not say the food was awful because the owners were paying for the advertorial.

I was recovering from an eye operation when Muttram interviewed me for *SuperMarketing* and I was wearing a bloodied eye patch. I suppose I was memorable, not necessarily for the right reasons, and Muttram showed his good judgment by hiring me—no doubt one of the attributes that assisted his meteoric rise to the top of Reed Business Information (RBI), *SuperMarketing*'s owner.

Muttram's modesty would probably preclude him from thinking of himself as a major influence on me, but he has been the proverbial angel on my shoulder for more than 30 years—my journalistic conscience, my professional moral compass—someone for whom I have enormous respect and affection. Muttram had my back, I felt—more or less—right from the start. He was also my harshest critic, especially if I got a bit too big for my boots and needed slapping down. We went to the pub together after work and sometimes at lunchtime, in the days when journalists had wet lunches. He knew how much I wanted to get out of features and into news and he helped me get there.

So it was that I became deputy news editor, and when Muttram became editor, he promoted me to the job I wanted most of all, news editor. It was a job that saw me come into my own and I found the confidence I had always lacked. It was a role that I felt made for. I loved it. It became my life.

Our tabloid newspaper style suited my news nose and under my news editorship we got better insight than the national dailies on the big grocery sector takeover stories of the day—Iceland v Bejam and Isosceles v Dee Corporation (Gateway)—BSE, salmonella in eggs, Sunday trading and South Africa and sanctions busting.

Every chance I got, I would thrust a copy of *SuperMarketing* into the hands of an unsuspecting politician, including then home secretary Douglas Hurd and the late Labour MP Bernie Grant (Tottenham, Lab) and photograph them holding our beloved organ. I breathed, ate and slept the publication.

When Ronald Reagan was US president, I got him to wave to a group of store managers I took to the US when we passed him in our coach. 'Hello Ron,' I yelled. He looked straight at us and waved. Ten years later the store managers were still talking about that trip and how 'Ronnie' waved to them.

I worked at *SuperMarketing* from November 1986 to October 1990 and, in that time, my confidence as a journalist bloomed. Even if not all of them liked me, my colleagues respected my news editor skills. Muttram rates me as the best news journalist he has worked with and I take great pride in that.

I finished my career on *SuperMarketing* as deputy editor—a role I did not like much. I wanted to be editor because that was the pinnacle, but my love was news editing—coming up with the news list, developing the news list as the week went on, briefing and guiding the reporters and then deciding what stories went where in the newspaper. I took editorial meetings when the editor was elsewhere, going through everything that we were all working on for the newspaper that week. The thought of taking editorial meetings previously terrified me. Now I revelled in it.

I did not want to be management, which was what deputy editor and editor roles effectively were, although I would have loved to have had the top editorial role on *SuperMarketing* briefly just to be able to say I had done it. I loved the hard mechanics of running a newspaper and that is what I did as news editor. I ran the show. I oversaw the nuts and bolts of putting everything together while the deputy editor and editor performed much wider roles that had more to do with management than editorial nitty-gritty. The editor and deputy editor roles were less about why I entered journalism—but, I figured, I had to climb the greasy pole into management positions to earn more money and status.

As a newsman, I had respect from chief executives in the food retail industry such as the late Sir Alistair Grant, even if they bristled at some of the stories we printed. Sir Alistair was close to thumping me when I got up on stage after he made a triumphant presentation at a high-level function and I questioned him about a member of his board whom suppliers always whinged about—probably because he was so good at his job screwing them down on price. His PR man, Tony Combes, called Claire Walker, *SuperMarketing's* editor at the time, and gave her an earbashing. I wouldn't have minded but it was her deputy, Jim Muttram, who briefed me to ask Sir Alistair the controversial question.

A year or so later, after I had my first article published in the *Financial Times*, a piece about product tampering by 'food terrorists', Sir Alistair approached me at a black-tie industry do and shook my hand. 'Congratulations,' he said. 'I read your article in the *FT*.' I appreciated that. He did not hold a grudge.

He said once that I reminded him of himself when Sir Jimmy Gulliver, founder of Argyll Foods, the company that took over Safeway in 1987, spotted him as a potential future chief executive. It was not many years later that Grant succumbed to the Big C. He died in 2001, aged just 63. I was greatly saddened.

Once, when I led on Iceland's takeover bid for Bejam I found myself on the same table as the frozen food retailer's chief executive, Malcolm Walker, and joint managing directors Peter Hinchcliffe and Richard Kirk, at an industry dinner during the height of the bid.

All hell had let loose when Iceland's board had discovered, before the function, that the deputy chairman of Bejam, Laurence Don, was my paternal uncle. Iceland's PR lady, Anne White, whom I knew well, insisted I was an objective journalist and my relationship to Laurence Don had no bearing on my coverage.

They must have been extra cautious that night but they were friend-ly to me and I was not made to feel uncomfortable in their presence.

I had always been tremendously proud of 'Uncle Laurie'. He was the only one of three siblings in a Polish immigrant family to rise to the dizzy heights of the board of a big shot PLC. Previously, he had been one of two management trainees alongside Ian MacLaurin at Tesco—now Lord MacLaurin—who went on to enjoy a spectacular career at the top of the supermarket group.

I had tried to keep my relationship to Laurence Don quiet at *Super-Marketing* because I did not want anyone to do me any special favours or try to use the fact we were related. I wanted to get to the top of my game on my own merits. I think I got respect from Jim Muttram and editor Claire Walker because I had deliberately kept that quiet and was visibly embarrassed when they asked me about it.

Early in 1990 Muttram's successor, Kate Trollope and I, now her deputy editor, fell victim to a shakeup, and a new publisher and editor were hauled in.

I had been thinking about going independent in any case because, while my title of deputy editor appealed to my ego, I stopped enjoying the job. All the politicking persuaded me it was time to fast-forward my plans—even more so when I heard, through the grapevine, about plans to turn our beloved tabloid-style publication into a features-ori-ented magazine in a bid to attract more advertising, and there would be no place for my brand of news.

I knew that was the beginning of the end of *SuperMarketing*, be-cause it just became an exceedingly poor 'me-too' to *The Grocer*. As a tabloid-style publication *SuperMarketing* had been distinctive and had its own voice and place in the market. People read it and advertised in it because of its hard, controversial and aggressive news edge with which I and my news team imbued it. I was right. It survived another couple of years and then RBI pulled the plug. It had lost not only its differentiation but its *raison d'etre*. The market did not need it.

Muttram, meanwhile, had been promoted to group editor of RBI's grocery group of publications, which included *Independent Retail News* and several sister titles, and when Trollope took over from him as editor of *SuperMarketing*, I missed reporting directly to him. We always had a great news rapport, bouncing ideas and angles off each other. But he was destined for high places and I knew he was quietly ambitious. One of the most intelligent men I have known, he impressed everyone he met with his intellect and his persuasive and calm, thoughtful argument.

You may not agree with him, but it was hard to argue against him—because whatever his view, he could argue for it with sound logic. Even if he won the argument, which he invariably did, he never made you feel you were stupid. I have never known someone who could be so convincingly diplomatic, and I am sure that is what impressed those at the top of parent group Reed Elsevier. Muttram climbed higher and higher in RBI when I became self-employed, ending up as managing director. I was enormously proud of him.

Muttram was full of great advice when I set up on my own in October 1990. At that time, the world of newspapers and magazines was transforming from typewriters, with their lovable clackety-clack keys and carbon paper, to the world of silent computers, which had a knack of crashing just as you hit deadline.

Muttram took charge of *Estates Gazette* and launched *Estates Gazette Interactive* (*EGi*) in the mid-late 1990s. He hired me in an independent capacity through his managing editor, Denis Hall, to offer a daily early-morning news service, which was to be delivered before people got into work.

I wrote my own contract with Muttram suggesting a few minor amendments. That contract sealed the deal of ever-increasing remuneration with annual increments in line with whichever index had risen most, the Retail Price Index or the Consumer Price Index.

Muttram's success with *EGi* led to him having great influence among others in the company and it was not long before I was also providing daily early-morning news services for *Farmers Weekly Interactive* and *Chemical News & Intelligence (CNI)*.

I also got in touch with another company called *Martin Information*, which provided news and intelligence from the hospitality, leisure and gaming industries. Peter Martin, the founder, later sold these services to William Reed Group, owner of *The Grocer*, *Convenience Store* and *Forecourt Retailer*, among others.

Martin had been advertising for a full-time member of staff, but I suggested to him he might be better off getting an experienced independent, arguing he would not have to pay various employment costs if he did so, plus he would get a really experienced journalist into the bargain. Martin knew of me by reputation and so began a successful ongoing business relationship. I secured an early-morning news service for *Martin Information*, too, and also news work during the day and weekend.

I sourced other independent journalists who did not mind working in the early hours—others like me—or shift-working national newspaper journalists. Soon, I had a roster of more than a dozen journalists I could call on. One used to work for me on the train while travelling home from his night shift on *The Sun*.

I managed all the news services and quality control, while keeping *EGi*, for the most part, to myself apart from, when I needed cover for illness and holidays, when an independent called Mike Read stepped into the breach and Clare O'Brien, an independent who had moved from Cambridgeshire to the West of Scotland.

It is rare for independent journalists to earn when they are on holiday unless they choose to write while away. Then it is not a holiday. But because I had a network of freelancers under me, I managed my margins carefully so that I made a reasonable, but not extortionate, sum on other people's work. I also ensured I paid them well and always quickly, which meant they were keen to help me out as and when needed.

The amount of margin added up and it was not long before my earnings topped £100,000 for seven years and there were many other years my income was in the high £70,000s, £80,000s and low £90,000s—not bad for someone writing out of a loft room. And my margins increased, too, because of the annual increase I had specified in my contracts with RBI.

This was a smart move because, in the case of *EGi*, I continued to produce its early-morning news service for 17 years, ultimately expanding it to a seven-days-a-week 364-days-a-year news service, eventually moving over to a 7am delivery time and directly imputing it using the content management system myself.

It was bloody hard work, during unsociable hours, when I should have been tucked up in bed, and sometimes the RBI clients could be difficult to deal with. Numerous times, I heard through my sources that they were reviewing the cost of outsourcing to me, but they would be persuaded by the quality they were getting and how important the service I supplied was to their overall model. Both Jim Muttram and also Denis Hall, when he was *EGi* managing editor, had my back.

Muttram's priority was the publications for which he was responsible—not our friendship—and that is how it should be. I supplied a great, consistent service and never let my clients down.

Muttram is now retired and we are still in touch. I have enormous respect for him and take all his advice and wisdom to heart. Over the years he has been honest with me. Once, when I had a job appraisal on *SuperMarketing* just before I became deputy news editor, he told me I needed to 'listen' more.

I do not think he appreciated at the time quite how bad my hearing was and I took it to heart. I worked on listening more rather than always interrupting. The concentration from working with my hearing problems and listening harder gave me headaches, but it was great advice which has served me well to this day, because if a journalist does not 'listen' they can miss the story altogether. And there was always paracetamol with caffeine for the headaches.

I thank my lucky stars for having met Jim Muttram. I do not think my life would have turned out so well if he had not interviewed me in 1986 for a job on *SuperMarketing*.

In brief

- A mentor is for life, not just for Christmas.

- Ensure your mentors feel appreciated and not used.

- Listen to your mentors even if you do not always like what you hear.

- As you gain experience, 'give back' to your mentors.

- One way of making decent money is to acquire a team of other freelance journalists that you subcontract for the kind of work that does not need you, specifically, to do all the donkey work. You just manage the quality/training. This can be sector-specific online news digests, contracting with trade associations or other bodies to publish their magazines, or operate as a middleman through which other journalists sell their stories.

- Do not keep all your eggs in one basket. Individual contracts rarely last a career's lifetime.

Chapter 5

Be the best at what you do

'Quality is not an act, it is a habit'

Aristotle

I am not the best journalist in the world. I am not even in the same universe as the Laura Kuenssbergs, the Kate Adies, the Jon Snows or Andrew Marrs.

What I had to offer clients was something that made me the best option for them when commissioning a specific editorial task and at a particular time. And I could always convince them of that. That is what I am good at. I believe I can do anything involving the English language. No one will dissuade me of that. I have specific attributes that make me a saleable commodity. You most likely will have, too. They might not be the same as mine, but if we all excelled at the same thing, we would not have the point of difference that attracts editors to us.

I believe I excel at:

- Getting a news angle out of anything.
- Spotting news angles where others insist none exist.

- Persuading others there is a news angle to be had where they cannot initially see one.

- Getting what I need to corroborate the news angle.

- Refusing to take 'no' for an answer.

- Never accepting defeat, while also rationalising and getting angry enough with rejection to maintain belief in myself to move on with the next thing or outlet and going on to sell.

- Knowing when enough is enough on research and interviewing and getting on with writing.

- Writing accurately and at speed.

- Treating each assignment as a profit centre and not sinking into loss (unnecessary excess hours spent researching, writing, dealing with clients). Balancing my workload by taking on news shifts (set fee) with features (payment per word) and longer-term editorial projects and independent editor roles (much more money).

- Managing others and getting them to make money for me. This is crucial if you have ambitions to retire on more than the state pension.

- An irrational fear of destitution (I was homeless briefly before I became a journalist).

Ask yourself what the things are that you excel at. Do you use them to maximise your income?

Play to your strengths. I did and I got great feedback from clients. Julian Westaway, who launched *Farmers' Weekly Interactive* (*FWi*), with me and my freelancers providing the early-morning news digest, was over the moon when *FWi* won RBI's award for best online service. He emailed me: 'Don's Hard News has been an essential part of our editorial content and I would like to thank you, and your team, for all your hard work in providing a highly reliable, professional service for *FWi*. I greatly appreciate the ease with which the service got off the ground and the consistency/reliability since launch. I regularly recommend you to other sites being developed and hope that some of these will result in more business in the future.'

When *Convenience Store* did not have a full headcount and I filled in with news stories, editor David Rees thanked me 'for your hard work and high-quality contribution during the period you have been on the team.'

Nic Robinson, then food and drink editor of the *Publican's Morning Advertiser*, emailed me his thanks when I turned around copy particularly quickly. Ronan Hegarty, news editor of *The Grocer*, wrote: 'I just wanted to say it has been great having you as part of the news team for the last 18 months and you've been a massive help to me during that time.'

Likewise, Damian Wild, then *Estates Gazette* editor, emailed me: 'I am grateful for the excellent service you have provided for so many years. It has served *EGi*—and our readers—well.'

Keep every congratulatory email you are sent. Such emails are great marketing tools to show prospective new clients how much editors appreciate you.

When asked what you do for a living, do not reply that you are a freelance. Freelance sounds tacky, unprofessional, like you do not mean it.

As a Mr John Osborne once advised me many years ago: 'You are not *just* a freelance. You are an independent freelance.' If you think of yourself as an independent you think of yourself more as a businessperson, and others do, too. Just a 'freelance' can be synonymous with a fly-by-night-just-bumming-around-until-I-get-a-real-job scenario.

Many independent journalists are martyrs to what they consider their art. That does not pay the gas bill, the kids' school fees or the mortgage. Journalists do not have to be martyrs. Many of us are highly principled and that is to the good, but we are running businesses at the end of the day. Think like a business and not like a freelance.

Within that parameter of being an independent businessperson, be the best independent businessperson in your specialist field—journalism, whether it is hard news, general features, specialist B2B, online content or all of those.

Ensure you are the first person the editor calls. Bang your own drum, publicise your skill on social media. You are the best at what you do. Really believe it. When pitching for a job, ask yourself, what is it I need to say in the first few lines that will convince the commissioner that I am the right person to write this? Others will believe it if you believe it. If they believe it, you will earn.

Belief that you are the best at what you do does not mean being arrogant. You can communicate that you are the best with humility. It is not about being a show-off. It is about being truthful about how good you are. I believe I am the best at what I have to offer. That is not being boastful. It is just how it is.

You clearly have skills if you have been an independent for five years and you have been invoicing £30,000-£40,000 each year. Taking this beyond £30,000-£40,000 requires more than just your editorial skills. It requires business know-how. So, if you want to hit six figures, as I did, think about how you can maximise the return from your labours. Brainstorm with yourself.

No one likes a bullshitter, and editors can spot one a mile off. Do not think you can pull the wool over an editor's eyes. They are usually editors for a reason, especially if they have worked their way up through the news ranks. A good news reporter gets a nose for bullshit. If you are going to argue you are brilliant and the best person for the job, you better had be otherwise you will never work for that publication again.

In brief

- Promote yourself as an independent rather than a freelance.

- Keep all correspondence in which clients have sung your praises and use to market yourself.

- Regard yourself as a business person as much as you are a journalist.

- Do not try to pull the wool over editors' eyes.

- Brainstorm with yourself—throw ideas around.

Chapter 6

It is not what you know, it is what people think you know

'There are things known and there are things unknown, and in between are the doors of perception'

Aldous Huxley

When I say that bullshit is a no-no, there is nothing wrong with letting people think you know far more than you do. This is not a contradiction. It is more of a nuance and I could carry it off because of my ability to research and ask the right questions of the right people.

I became an expert in the field of multiple grocery retailing and diversified into affiliated subjects that were related to the sector or substrata of it, such as property, legal matters, employment issues, technology, communications, small business, general retail, hairdressing, hospitality and travel. Think of a game of word association and before long I was writing about anything and everything. I was not a specialist in everything I wrote about, but I had the skills to write articles that were of interest to specialists and told them something new or gave them a different perspective.

Between 1997 and 1999 I got a lot of kudos writing for *FT Food Business* and I went through a period, from the turn of the millennium, when I wrote prolifically for the nationals—personal finance features for *The Observer Cash*, for example, features for *The Guardian's G2* and *Times 2*, the odd piece for the *FT*, *The Telegraph*, news pieces for the tabloids. It was then that I felt I had avenged myself against Jim Wardlaw who had done so much to undermine my fragile self-confidence and my prospects as a journalist when I was training at the *Fleet Street News Agency*.

I could not be an expert in lots of areas the way, for example, some people focus on beer, or on wine. I do not have it in me to write about single subject areas as an independent journalist, because I have a low boredom threshold.

Why should an editor or section head hire me to write about something in which I am not expert? Because it is not what you know but what they think you know and their faith in your ability to produce what it is they require. If you have come up with the goods for them previously then they will keep coming back.

That way I have written authoritative pieces on subjects as diverse as genetically modified food and drug addiction, and across many styles of writing, such as a Christmas pantomime for *Hairdressers' Journal International—Hairlarious on Ice*, and another, which was a skit on *The Lion King*, featuring King Crimper with songs such as *Hairkuna Haircutta*. They will not get me a West End debut but who cares? Someone was willing to pay me for them.

A little bit of knowledge on many, many subjects can go a long way and insulate you against hard times more than expertise in a single topic.

Research your pitch, craft it and then fire at your target.

Your succinct, well-informed pitch should look like you know what you are talking about or, at least, illustrate a desired direction of travel.

It should demonstrate you know how to make the subject appealing and that you have the wherewithal to ask the right questions and ask them of the right people.

I always tell people you do not have to be an expert in subjects you write about. You should just have an insatiable appetite to find the experts who will give you the facts and opinions that will turn your writing into an expertly-written news article, opinion column or feature.

When I worked for *SuperMarketing*, I built up an unsurpassed contacts book. By the time I left, I had about 10 boxes of card files, and if anyone on the newspaper needed a suggestion of whom to speak to about any given subject within grocery, they would come to me.

It is partly because of my contacts that *SuperMarketing* continued to hire me as an independent. With my departure went a pool of industry knowledge that could not be hired anywhere else. I left a vacuum, and the new publisher knew it. Therein lay an opportunity.

Big-shot City food retail analysts wined and dined me because they knew how well connected I was.

But I did not want to be pigeon-holed when I became independent, so I pitched far and wide. In the early years, I wrote a feature about complementary medicine, one on designing offices for company directors, another on duty-free shopping, another on hiring au pairs, one on children with special educational needs, autobiographical pieces about my own life experiences, features about parenting, and euthanasia, a book on stillbirth and miscarriage.

I believe the new publisher of *SuperMarketing*, Gary Noble, quickly understood why I was sometimes feared and respected by those who were the subjects of my news stories and he appreciated my news ability. Noble was also publisher of *Hairdressers' Journal International* (*HJi*), another RBI magazine, and he hauled me in as an independent to shake up its news coverage when it was a weekly magazine.

I was not a hairdressing expert. Split Enz was a great little Ozzie band and that was about as much as I knew. I rarely got my hair cut and my memories of barbers were visiting the old-fashioned type in North Wembley with my father where a table was stacked high with mucky mags and the cut rounded off with a question as to whether Sir would like something for the weekend. I should be so lucky!

I turned *HJi* on its head with hard politics-based news stories. It may surprise those who do not know the hairdressing market, but few other industries are more political, especially in the competition world—and on the back of my stories, people in the industry assumed I was an expert. Why should I let them think any different? Like I say, it is not what you know but what people think you know.

On the strength of my *HJi* work, I got work for *Salon Business*, did some newsletters at different times for hair products manufacturers Wella and L'Oreal and became founding editor of *SalonFocus,* on an independent basis.

From knowing nothing, I quickly got under the skin of the industry and rapidly developed a network of contacts who knew everything that was going on. I knew those in the sector that were business experts and those who were long-hair, short-hair, curly-hair and colour specialists, and a trichologist who knew all about baldness.

In next to no time, I had the mobile and home numbers of Toni Mascolo, late chief of Toni & Guy, and other leading celebrity stylists.

No one loves a good chat more than hairdressers. It was wonderful to be able to define news on my own terms in a sector of business journalism not known for its news content. I kept detached so I did not feel obligated to anyone.

It was all about my contacts and getting them to confide in me. Hairdressers love a bit of a yarn and some can be prone to go off-subject a lot because they are generally extrovert and loquacious, so I had to really use my journalistic skills to separate fact from hearsay. I had to be scrupulous in my fact checking. As I moved from grocery, to hairdressing, to property to personal finance, as the years went by, I could only be an expert on a per-piece basis, based on my research and my ability to find the right people to talk to on any given topic.

My old grocery contacts moved on or died. The structure of the industry changed and, as I was writing about so many different subjects to keep the money coming in, I ceased to be the best-connected journalist in grocery, just as I later ceased to be one of the best-connected journalists in hairdressing and on and on it goes as I switched from subject to subject, like a cuckoo switching nests.

I continued to write news remotely for *The Grocer* four days a week as an independent right up until my move to Wales and did the odd bit of work for *The Grocer*, *Independent Retail News* and *Fleet News* after my move, but when I wanted to, rather than out of necessity.

I was always *The Grocer* news editor Ronan Hegarty's first pick from a pool of independents because I generated my own leads. I happily chased down stories they tipped me off about, too, and contributed historical perspective, having written on and off about the sector for so many years; some of my old contacts were still in the industry and I made new contacts.

The Grocer often liked me to work on wholesale and convenience stories, and I generated a whole new library of contacts for the period I worked for the magazine. That was one of my strengths: making new contacts, recording all those contacts and getting them to give me news tips and trust me all at the same time.

You do not get £100,000-plus of work writing for one publication four days a week. I did other assignments before hours, after hours, late into the night, over the weekend. There were not enough hours in the day.

Between all that, I managed to find time to adopt two children, rear an assortment of dogs, cats and a parrot, and keep in touch with friends acquired from schooldays.

What I learned was, you can do whatever you believe you can do. If you believe it, you can make other people believe it. You perform and it is a self-fulfilling prophecy.

I worked like a demon and balanced it with all other aspects of my personal life. I did not get much sleep. This does take a toll and during the noughties my thyroid gave out on me and I became ill but, still, I slaved away even though I could barely move one foot in front of the other.

My GP told me I had the worst case of an auto-immune form of hypothyroidism his group practice had seen but, once diagnosed, I was put on medication, and I was soon running up and down the stairs again to my attic office.

In brief

- A little bit of expertise on many subjects rather than focusing on one can insulate you for the long term.

- Asking the right questions can persuade people you know more than you do.

- Your pitch should be crafted—a work of art.

- Develop a knack for approaching the right interviewees who will help make your articles authoritative.

- A continuously updated contacts book/database is your best asset.

- Work all hours and weekends.

- You can do whatever you believe you can do.

Chapter 7

Reinvent the wheel

'Everyone thinks of changing the world, but no one thinks of changing himself'

Leo Tolstoy

I have continually reinvented myself.

Firstly, there were the post-*SuperMarketing* years when I could trade off my reputation gained writing about multiple food retailing.

I was fresh off the newspaper and everyone who was anyone in the grocery trade knew me as did all the editors and journalists. My reputation in the sector at that time was second to none.

I wrote for a vast array of food publications: *SuperMarketing*, *The Grocer*, *Frozen & Chilled Foods*, *Fish Trader*, *Fish & Chips* and *Fast Food*, *Caterer & Hotelkeeper*, *The Publican*, the *Morning Advertiser*, *Food FIPP*, *Independent Retail News*, *Convenience Store* and many, many more. I was business editor of *ProWholesaler*, the publication of the Federation of Wholesale Distributors and business editor of *Asian Business*, where I had a regular column. Several PR companies hired me on a consultancy basis to advise them on client magazines.

You would be amazed how many food-focused publications there were back then. I got calls from editors in the US who asked me to write 'expert' pieces, such as on petrol forecourt retailing and a US newsletter called *Food & Drink Daily* in the early 1990s asked me to provide them with daily news stories. I was able to recycle other material I had written and researched for UK publications and knock them out in half-an-hour, on top of whatever else I was working on at the time. It was all this multitasking that made my earnings accrue.

But, I was scared: I knew that I was stretching my knowledge over many areas of the food industry when my expertise had been specifically about the supermarket arena. I realised that my knowledge and contacts would become diluted over time and that I would increasingly have to become a Jack of all trades. That was the only way I would survive as a self-employed businessman for the long-term—thirty years as it turned out—and remedy my low-boredom threshold.

I did not think I would be able to generate enough work becoming world expert in supermarkets long term, nor did I want to. There was more to life and writing than Tesco and baked beans—as fascinating as they were—and believe me, they were fascinating. The more you get into a seemingly narrow topic, the more you realise it is bigger than you think.

There is huge satisfaction becoming world expert on a niche sector. I was interviewed on TV, on radio and frequently called upon by national newspaper journalists to help them out with sector-specific stories.

Just after I left *SuperMarketing*, I managed to sell a few food retailing news stories to John Thornhill, who was then the *FT*'s food retail guru. The *FT* did not take stories from *anybody*. You had to have a trustworthy reputation because the 'pink'un' valued accuracy above all else.

I had a reputation among other trade press colleagues. When I met them at Christmas parties for the first time, they would say 'so *you're* Andrew Don'—[so and so] 'says you're the best news journalist they've worked with.' Not the best food retailing journalist but the best *news* journalist. I liked that.

Thousands of independents churn out features, and I have done thousands of such features during my career, but you do not earn big money just knocking out features for the trade press—not even the nationals, unless you happen to get a regular *Daily Mail* slot or are a celebrity journalist. I was no celebrity and had no desire to be.

My supermarket sector expertise diminished as the mid-1990s went into the new millennium. However, what did not diminish were my news skills and my ability to write about anything at any time, at speed, well within deadline and for people to assume, from what I wrote, that I was an expert.

And so, it was at different times I wrote about hairdressing as a business rather than as an art and became managing editor of a well-respected magazine for the casual food dining market, *Peach Report*. Here, it was my editing skills that I was hired for—and not my knowledge of the sector. This, Peter Martin, who hired me had in spades and I doubt many could come anywhere near his knowledge of the casual dining market.

By association with *Peach Report*, everyone assumed I was a sector expert. I was not. What I was, was a bloody good sub-editor and rewriter. On the back of *Peach Report*, I got lots of work for specialist publications in the hospitality industry.

Peach Report was a magazine I could put to press while working on lots of other stuff. I picked my hours and juggled multiple assignments to boost my earnings.

When I was launch editor of *SalonFocus*, the National Hairdressers' Federation's (NHF) magazine, I also wrote the president's annual conference speeches. I edited the trade association's '*Strategy for the 21st Century*' and its annual reports for a good many years. I was confidante to general secretary Eileen Lawson and advised on PR strategy and wrote press releases on a retainer. All these things boosted my income because I did them alongside other assignments.

As editor of *SalonFocus*, I encapsulated 'it is not what you know, it is what people think you know'. Babtac, a trade association for the beauty industry in those days, asked me to write a regular two-page 'column' for its magazine. I knew F-all about beauty, despite a stint writing news for *Professional Beauty*, but Babtac did not know that. As I say, it is not what you know, it is what people think you know. All you need is the ability to research quickly and ask the right questions.

In brief

- Recycle your previously used material.
- Be prepared to write about anything and everything as well as any specialist areas.
- Become known for your expertise in your specialist areas.
- Try to get the right mix of work that enables you to maximise your income.
- Learn to juggle multiple assignments.
- Branch out into other writing areas such as speeches.

- Work on others' perception of you.

- The ability to research quickly and ask the right questions is essential.

Chapter 8

Be your harshest taskmaster

'A great man is hard on himself; a small man is hard on others'

Confucius

Be the independent that editors want to fight for. No one respects a pushover. Fight for your rights but also know when it is the right time to back down.

Never forget that you are supplying a service just like a restaurant supplies a dining experience. Your customers are royalty. Love them, nurture them, cherish them. They pay your electric bill. You need them. It does not matter that you might regard some as douche bags. Bite your tongue and think of next autumn's holiday in the Seychelles.

I ensured I always delivered ahead of deadline and met every aspect of the brief, or the pitch, as it had been accepted. I ensured, where appropriate, every feature had strong news angles that made my commissioning editors sit up.

You have to keep delivering quality day in and day out to be a serious long-term independent. You cannot have an off-day. I recall times when working for *EGi*, I would deliver its early-morning news service with a sick bucket next to my desk because it was too late to get cover from one of my networks of independents.

I suffered from Meniere's Disease and could get an attack when it was too late to get cover. I could not turn around to *EGi* managing editor Denis Hall, and later, *Estates Gazette* editor Damian Wild and say: 'Sorry, I couldn't deliver today, I was ill.' They had subscribers who did not want to know the journalist who delivered their news was incapacitated. They wanted what they paid for and quite right, too.

I could have been on the sinking Titanic without Wi-Fi, mobile signal or lifeboat and I probably would have tied my copy to one of my parrot's legs. My badge of honour in all my years as a journalist is to never have let an editor down. It is a record of which I am justifiably proud.

For every feature I was commissioned I always gave them a hard news edge where appropriate and lived up to my trading name—*Don's Hard News*. Sometimes, I would also take some of the news angles I got and turn them into individual stories for other publications. In an industry increasingly riven with copyright grabs—where publications insist you relinquish your legal ownership of your work—and other restrictive terms and conditions, I had to do this in a way that did not piss off any customers.

The only time I have ever got seriously irate with a publishing company was when I shot the messenger who asked me to sign an indemnity contract just over a year before my move to Wales. I was one of several independents who were sent ultimatums to either sign over copyright and indemnify the publisher or do one—not exactly in those words, but it was made clear that those who did not sign would not be able to work for the company.

I have decided not to name this company because I get on famously with its editors and section heads and what it asked its independents to do is, sadly, not uncommon nowadays.

I phoned HR and left an angry message on voicemail, all the more narked that no one answered the phone. It did not go down well. I was in a tricky position because I also wrote for many of the company's other titles. In the end, through gritted teeth, I signed and increased my libel cover. I would advise everyone to get libel cover. All it can take is one legal action to evaporate your dreams of a comfortable retirement. You cannot rely on the publication you write for to foot the bill.

I would always advise others to resist agreeing to indemnify publications. If they are prepared to hire you, they must be prepared to cover you in case of legal action as long as you are not reckless.

However, in the odd isolated case it may be prudent to be pragmatic and give in to customers' demands. I earned back the extra cost in libel cover many times over from the work I got from said company and carried on paying into my pension. I refused to indemnify some other publishing groups. Some did not use me again. On copyright, others were happy for me to retain this as long as I granted them a licence to reuse my work. Most would not pay extra for this licence but, again, it was a case of what served me best for the long haul.

I believe the blitz on independent journalists' rights is an outrage. No one should give away copyright unless they are paid a reasonable fee for that copyright. Independent journalists should not have to indemnify their customers in case of a libel action if the journalist can demonstrate they have not been reckless.

I was often hired because I took on the more difficult stories—the ones that could potentially end up on the arse of legal action, so to ask me to indemnify them was a tad rich.

This is an area I feel needs regulatory intervention. No independent should ever feel coerced into giving up copyright and indemnifying their customers for fear of being blacklisted or losing work.

The Authors' Licensing and Collecting Society (ALCS) is money for old rope. For the couple of minutes it takes to register each of your published journal articles online it throws money at you once, or twice a year, for your secondary rights—fees academic institutions and others pay to photocopy your work. The ALCS can be a lucrative source of income just for a couple of minutes registering each published journal article on its database.

Its website has a tick box which asks whether the journalist retains the copyright of articles they register online or that they have an agreement in place with their publisher to claim secondary rights. No publishing company should try to deny an independent of the right to claim from ALCS.

I have earned thousands from this over the years and high four-figures in a single year. It is like having Dire Straits' *Money for Nothing* on repeat.

The amount can vary considerably each year depending on when fees are collected and from whom by the time of totting up the disbursement. The fees earned from ALCS has helped swell my pension, paid for holidays and covered expenditure during slow months.

The journalist who consistently delivers, not just what the editor wants but above and beyond, stands a better chance of getting the terms and conditions they want.

It may not be enough, however, because the editors are restrained by higher management and directors but at least you might get the editor fighting your corner. Freelance journalists are ten a penny. Be the independent that editors want to fight for. No one respects a pushover. Fight for your rights but also know when it is the right time to back down. When I look at the volume and value of invoices paid by the companies I gave in to, I know I made the right decision. Martyrs end up dead, after all.

In brief

- Resist indemnifying publishers and assigning copyright.
- Fight for your rights but know when to back down.
- Your customers pay the bills—treat them like royalty.
- Never EVER let anyone down.
- Deliver added value.
- Never be reckless.
- Sign up with ALCS—it's money for old rope.
- Be the independent that editors want to fight for.
- Martyrs end up dead.

Chapter 9

Love your IT guru

'Technology is cool, but you've got to use it as opposed to letting it use you'

Prince

Your most important asset is your IT guru, especially if, like me, computer meltdown turns your bowels to mush when on deadline. This is another good reason for filing copy in good time because, as a wise person once said, 'If shit can happen, it will.' Therefore, I have at least two of everything IT-related.

If there is one golden nugget which every independent journalist should emblazon across their soul, it is to get the best IT guru available. Love them, nurture them, send them a hamper every Christmas and make them part of your family.

An IT guru who is there like magic, remotely logging onto your computer and fixing all manner of ills in front of your eyes when you need them, is a joy to behold.

Press Gazette ran a profile on me when I was 34, headlined *[My] technophobia*. That was then. Nowadays, I often troubleshoot other people's computer problems. I conquered my fear and picked up some skills, but I cannot do everything.

From time to time, I will call on my technology angel, whom I first came across at RBI. Mike was instrumental in helping the company switch from typewriters and carbon paper to the world of tech in 1990.

I was one of the first journalists at RBI to switch to a computer. I desperately missed the clackety-clack of the typewriter keys, the comforting motion of whacking the carriage-return lever and the intoxicating sound of pulling the typewritten sheet from the roller, scrunching the paper, aiming it at the bin and hitting Paul Braithwaite, the chief sub, instead (accidentally on purpose).

Suddenly there was something called ASCII Save. I used a word processing programme called Websters and used a modem (a communications device to transfer data digitally) to send copy via what sounded like a series of bleeps and farts.

The new technology seemed to change almost monthly. My head spun. I tried to keep pace because I knew the future was digital, and I knew it would be an intrinsic part of my future success.

I had previously prevailed on a friend before I tracked down Mike. David serviced my car, put up shelves in my office, fixed the vacuum cleaner and demolished my mother-in-law's asbestos air-raid shelter.

I am grateful to David for all the help he gave me, often well after midnight, but he was the equivalent of the car mechanic sourcing parts from the breakers yard to save money—which he did also.

I remember the numerous late nights when David would dictate nonsensical auto-exec.bat strings and registry changes over the phone, which made me tremble as I inputted, fearing my machine would spontaneously combust.

Windows 3.11 was a nightmare with more crashes than the Grand Prix. Then came the viruses, malware and—thank God—Mike, who understood the journalist mindset.

He went above and beyond—sometimes troubleshooting my computer in the early hours before I began my early-morning news shifts, when everything had to be working pristinely. I owe my IT guru everything. I lacked patience. I did not want to waste the hours it could take troubleshooting a computer problem because that was lost hours when I could be earning. It was a distraction. Yet, it was watching Mike remotely access my computer and observing what he did with the cursor that taught me how to troubleshoot many of my own problems.

Computer problems played havoc with my mental stability. A misbehaving computer was the ultimate panic inducer. My mind would race: would I be destitute? Would the computer ever be fixed? Would I have to buy a new machine and what was to stop that one crashing? I could not sleep. What if I broke my record of always delivering for my customers? Computer havoc made me feel I was out of control. Something I did not understand controlled my anxiety levels.

There was only one thing to do—buy several computers so if one went down, at least I had another. I used off-site servers to back up as well as portable hard drives, Redundant Array of Inexpensive Disks (RAID) to protect me from disc deaths and it was an electricity supply issue that introduced me to Uninterrupted Power Supplies (UPSs) after a power cut corrupted my hard drive.

Have more than one computer, use a cloud backup like Dropbox, iCloud or OneDrive and pay the annual fee that enables you to back up all your files to it so that if shit happens, the worst you will need to do is copy all your files over from your cloud storage, minimising downtime and client disappointment. Pay for the best computer security you can and always apply security updates.

My advice to any independent journalist is to try to learn as much as you can about technology. Although you are a journalist and not a computer guru, technology has become so intertwined with every aspect of the job and life generally that you need to be comfortable with it. I learned the hard way. But at least I learned.

I had a two-year stint on *Drinks Marketing*, a monthly magazine housed in a building next to *The Telegraph*, in Fleet Street, between working at the Fleet Street News Agency and Middlesex County Press. It comprised a three-man editorial team and both the editor, Tony Warner, and deputy editor, Mike Dennis, took me under their wing and gave me the opportunity to further develop my news skills on press day when they would let me off my leash to track down exclusive news stories. One was an angle on the Brixton Riots. I got a tremendous buzz from news even though my main job for the rest of the month was to write features about subjects such as Spanish wine and white spirits.

I got to know the drinks industry well, went to many pretentious wine tastings where wine snobs proclaimed in look-at-me-aren't-I-superior voices that a vile white had floral notes with nutty nuances. Still, I could bullshit with the rest of them, especially when I was inebriated. Everyone else spat. I swallowed.

At one of my first interviews, with a director of Hedges & Butler, I forgot to switch my tape recorder on and had not taken notes. I had a panic attack when I realised and started shaking. My interviewee took pity on me and he ran through everything for a second time. No one has ever heard that story until now because I was so embarrassed. It is an important lesson for all journalists. Even when I first started using a computer, I still had a Smith Corona Golf Ball typewriter for an emergency and a fax machine.

I never relied on technology again without a backup. You might have the most expensive sophisticated digital recorder but take notes at the same time—just in case. Hopefully, you will have mastered your 100 words/minute shorthand.

My degree of hearing loss made a combination of recordings and scribbles essential, and I always managed to scribble my way through phone interviews with lots of F's for Freddie and S's for sugar. It was harder for me than for most getting shorthand notes down because it took all my concentration to decipher mumbled voices.

Finally, I cannot recommend email that is stored in the cloud highly enough so that your email is synced on all your devices. Your email client is your filing cabinet and will contain a goldmine of information and records over the years. You really do not want to lose it.

In brief

- Get a sympathetic IT guru who understands deadlines and make them feel appreciated.
- Have two of everything.
- Use the cloud and portable hard drives.
- Install a Redundant Array of Inexpensive Disks (RAID).
- Use Uninterrupted Power Supplies (UPSs).
- Learn all you can about technology so you can troubleshoot your own problems.
- If using a recording device, make notes at the same time.

Chapter 10

Belt and braces

'If we are wise, let us prepare for the worst'

George Washington

I started writing this before Coronavirus took over from Brexit as the word that came up in every other sentence. Many parts of the UK were reeling from storms Ciara and Dennis. Homes and businesses were flooded, and lives were turned upside down. Little did we know that COVID-19 was about to dramatically change all our lives.

Imagine that you ran your business from one of those storm-wrecked properties. Did you opt for the cheapest home insurance quote you could find, or did you opt for a belt-and-braces policy, such as from Hiscox or John Lewis that would get you up and running as quickly as you could say 'deadline'?

The worst may never happen to you. But it might.

I appreciate that spending money on insurance feels like putting cash into a black hole and, in a way, it is, but if the shit hits the fan, the black hole becomes gold. Get the best insurance you can afford. Read the wording. How are their claims handling? Do they cover a 'home office'? Will all your tools of the trade be covered?

One of the attributes a professional independent journalist should have is financial nous. Pay for quality. Insurance is no difference from overseas holidays in that the general rule is you get what you pay for.

I recommend insuring to the hilt if you can afford to, even if you never need to claim. You are paying for peaceful sleep at night. Spend the time reading policy small print and never mind that it is brain-numbing and tedious.

No two policies are the same. Compare like with like and do not buy on price. Buying insurance on price alone is like buying a second-hand computer that is full of malware. It will come back to bite.

Pensions are another area many people pay too little thought to when they become self-employed. New independents have other priorities. I get it, but you will regret it as your 60s approach and all you have to look forward to is a meagre state pension and that is only if you have paid at least 35 years' worth of National Insurance contributions.

A summer's day feels like an eternity to children. Individual days will linger in their long-term memories and stand out sharply over the course of time, which passes more quickly the older we become—not in real terms as far as we measure time, but it is as if our brains respond to time differently. We seem to be able to achieve much more when we are younger, get more tasks done in a day and we have greater energy to complete them.

When we grow older, it feels like an hour goes too quickly, as does the day, the week, the month and the year. One Christmas rolls into another. Before you know it you are knackered and you are not so resilient.

Those who have been attuned to the financial services sector and have bothered to understand it and have taken the best advice available will be able to ease off if they so wish by the time they start to feel their age—or older!

Somehow, jumping out of bed at 5am when you are 55 is not as easy as it was when you were 20 when you somehow managed to burn the candle at both ends.

Now that I am in my late-50s, I appreciate life lasts but a moment. When you are suffering, the pain seems to go on for ever. When you look back, however, you wonder where all the time went. You may think winding down or that semi-or-total-retirement is decades away if you are in your 20s and have just become self-employed. But it might be further away than you think. Indeed, you might never be able to retire.

The trend is for the state pension age to be getting later and later as we live into our 80s and 90s and reaching 100 is not as unusual as it once was. We have a pension crisis. Do you want to spend your retirement years counting your pennies or do you want to be able to go on holidays and eat out a couple of times a week without worrying whether you can pay your household bills?

No one can live the life of Riley on the state pension if they live long enough to receive it. Fail to consider retirement when you are young and you might have to work until you drop. Many people do—some out of choice, but how awful it would be if you wanted to retire or strike a better work-life balance but could not afford to. The state pension allows for bare subsistence—not financial freedom.

A private pension is essential for quality of life—not next year, or the year after. Start saving for your retirement now. Your financial adviser, like your IT guru, will be your best friend. Find one you can trust and plough as much of your earnings into it as you can. If your earnings increase, invest more. If they decrease, invest less. Increase or decrease your contributions according to fluctuations in your earnings.

I was paying £1,700 net a month into my pension at my peak earnings. Prevailing tax rules meant the government added 25% on top. Just before I escaped the rat race, I was paying £300, at other times I paid £750. I was able to adjust it according to what I could afford. Aged 57 I had accrued enough wealth to apply the brakes on my 12-plus hour days.

A lot of people I speak to worry that putting money into a pension is too big a sacrifice. After all, they might get cancer or break their neck skiing before they can claim it. But they might also get to 70 and kick themselves.

Choosing the right financial adviser who understands your attitude to risk is essential. Find a financial adviser who makes sense. Avoid the ones who speak in financial clichés. Quiz them as you would anyone else while interviewing for a story. If they cannot explain stuff in language a two-year-old can understand, they probably do not know what they are talking about. Apply your journalistic skills and you will not go far wrong.

Do your best to understand how pensions work. I used to panic in a financial crisis when stock markets plunged. But I quickly learned that is exactly the time when you invest, because you get more widgets for your money which, on an upturn, will ensure you are quids in. Short of nuclear war, there is always an upside—even during a pandemic.

Another thing to think about is how to protect your assets. When you first become self-employed, your only assets might be a computer and the shirt on your back, but if you are a success that will change. What happens if you are sued for libel and you lose? The publishing company you worked for should cough up in my opinion, but remember those horrible indemnity clauses I mentioned earlier? Do not lose the roof over your head and jeopardise your future—get a writers' policy. I never had to claim on it, but it saved me sleepless nights.

Critical illness cover is desirable and will pay out a lump sum, and income protection policies will cover you for loss of pay should you be out of action, due to ill health for an extended period—usually starting from four to six weeks after you are no longer able to work. Critical illness cover is one of those apparent black holes I referred to earlier. Let us hope you never have to claim on it. But I have known colleagues who have got critical illnesses when relatively young and were not covered. Such cover takes a lot of financial pressure off loved ones or might help you realise a bucket list.

I have had private medical insurance (PMI) virtually from birth thanks to the foresight of my father, and I have never been without it. While I have had many operations on the NHS, the beauty of PMI is that you can usually get treated much more quickly, although not necessarily any better, and have a wider net of surgeons and hospitals from which to choose. Throw in the private room and you can be up and working on your laptop as soon as you come around from the anaesthetic, if you feel inclined to do so.

PMI is horribly expensive. It starts off affordable but the older you get the more expensive it becomes. If, along the way, you fall victim to several conditions, these become pre-existing conditions, which may prevent you going for a cheaper policy with another provider if you want those conditions covered.

Home rental is a mug's game, although, unfortunately, many people have this as their only option. Get on the housing ladder as early as you can and use lucrative periods to pay off more than the required amount. My wife and I bought our house for £153,000 in 1995.

Abbey National, as it was then known, persuaded us to take out an endowment/interest-only mortgage. Fortunately, a few years in I had the foresight to realise the endowment was never going to pay off the mortgage and that all the promises about having a big lump of cash to boot, after the endowment supposedly paid off the mortgage, was fantasy.

I swiftly changed to a repayment mortgage with another provider and paid off more than the required amount each month, as well as lump sums when my earnings were particularly good.

A few years before moving to Wales, I had paid off the mortgage and subsequently sold my house for a 470% profit. And as my wife and I owned 100% equity in the house, it was this equity windfall, a move to a part of the UK where house prices are much cheaper yet the environment far more enriching and nurturing, plus the option to draw down from our pensions at whatever point in the future we chose, that gave us the chance to live a more fulfilling life.

I am not a union man—not in the sense of The Strawbs' *Part of the Union*. Going on strike! Forget it. I have, nonetheless, been a member of the NUJ for more years than I care to remember. A trade union can help when the worst happens. The NUJ's magazine *The Journalist*, is worth getting. The Union has occasionally helped me with work issues and queries, although I feel it needs to accomplish more on the issue of publishers' strong-arming independents into relinquishing their copyright and forcing them into signing indemnification clauses.

In brief

- Shit happens.
- Imagine the worst that could happen and insulate yourself from it as far as you reasonably can.
- Get the best insurance you can afford.
- Read the small print.
- Get a private pension plan and put away as much as you can *today*.
- As we get older, time goes faster, we get less done, our energy decreases.
- Find a trustworthy financial adviser whom you gel with.
- Get a writers' policy, consider medical insurance, critical illness and income protection.
- If you have money to spare, overpay your mortgage.
- Join the NUJ's freelance branch.

Chapter 11

The social media viper pit

'Why is it that people with the most narrow of minds
seem to have the widest of mouths?'

Lewis Carroll

I am not great at social media. There are plenty of other resources for independent journalists to learn about how to make social media work for them, but even a lapsed technophobe such as I have used Twitter, Facebook and LinkedIn for researching stories and contacting people.

Some people respond more quickly to a Tweet, a Facebook or WhatsApp message, a LinkedIn post or a text than to an email. I have picked up work through Twitter. Indeed, I found the publisher of this book through Twitter. The social media platform helps keep my 'brand' in the line of sight of anyone who is interested enough to follow.

Social media enables independents to show their human side. They are no longer faceless.

My profile information on Facebook is deliberately incorrect. This is because I do not trust putting my date of birth and other personal details online and I am staggered by those who do. I am from the generation that does not trust technology and my natural journalistic instinct is to be paranoid about data security.

If you are one of those who does not have the problems I have with social media, then I am sure it will enhance your working life far more than it has enhanced mine, as long as it is not 'noise'—a distraction. It is all too easy when struggling to get hold of people to let social media distract. Likes and retweets produce an endorphin rush. It validates you and your opinions, especially when those who like or retweet your post have gravitas and lots of followers/friends. Who does not feel just a little bit validated when a celebrity with hundreds of thousands of followers retweets them? It is far better to take the dog for a walk in the fresh air and clear your head if you need a distraction.

Frivolous use of social media during 'normal' office hours might prompt your customers to reflect on what kind of a journalist you are if you can spend your time cursing Donald Trump when one of their staff has commissioned you to write about the decline of the high street.

Or it might make others think that you cannot have much work and therefore cannot be much of a journalist if you have time to write frivolous posts.

It can also be dangerous. Never, *never* post after drinking alcohol. You may live to regret it. Avoid nastiness. Do not become one of the loudmouth bully-types prevalent on social media. Using a public platform comes with responsibility just as writing for a newspaper or magazine does. Do not let yourself down. Careers can be destroyed or hampered with a single ill-advised post. Libel laws apply just as much online as they do in print.

Never forget that while social media can be a great platform for the independent journalist, to provide links to published stories and as an overall marketing showcase, it has an Achilles' heel.

Be cognisant that people love those who are self-effacing. I will happily take the piss out of myself and admit to hypocrisy, although changing one's mind does not necessarily amount to hypocrisy.

Most journalists do not grasp that politicians can change their minds on issues, too. It does not make those people hypocrites or unreliable. It may just be that others' arguments have swayed them, or new evidence persuaded them to think differently.

It could mean they are open-minded; they are people who listen, they use their intellect to accept that their first thoughts on something can change. Us journalists love headlines that scream 'U-turn'—as black and white as that. My colleagues, especially on the tabloids, often find it hard to accept there are nuances—shades of grey.

Social media could also be called 'visible media' because we expose ourselves to one and all when we use it. We sacrifice an element of our privacy. If we are to be visible 24 hours a day, we need to make sure we are showing our best side to our customers or the side that will best promote our work.

I have been guilty along with most of posting Tweets that are a cry of frustration at political events. We all do it and there is nothing wrong in that—in what we believe to be an open and democratic society. But, if you do so, just have an eye to your followers, especially if they are mostly business contacts.

You might just want to think about deleting those old Tweets in which you likened Vladimir Putin to Mr Potato Head or Xi Jinping to a shrivelled water chestnut if you are going to Russia or China on assignment. Social media posts can come back to haunt.

I have always regarded myself as a maverick. So, if I were to Tweet that Boris Johnson is a big girls' blouse, which these days is a bit politically incorrect, it probably would not have done me any harm because my customers know I can be provocative.

The negative about social media is that you are putting yourself out there and you can become a target.

Facebook has been particularly useful for trying to get hold of people who do not have a website, and micro businesses that, bizarrely, do not publish their correct phone number.

I would message them on Facebook, and I would often get a quick reply. This frequently happened for a magazine I wrote for in the three years before moving to Wales called *Fine Food Digest*. Some of the people I needed to contact might be making a top-notch artisan delicacy at home and they were harder to get hold of on the phone.

LinkedIn is a great place to publish links to your articles. Write a comprehensive profile and it is a brilliant tool for prospective editors to size you up. I have not posted much on LinkedIn or Facebook, but I have found my LinkedIn profile to be incredibly useful when pitching for assignments. People I often want to talk to might research me first on LinkedIn before picking up the phone to me—just to check I am who I say I am.

My own website is the equivalent of a car showroom. Here you can learn everything you need to know about my working life. I provide hypertext links to the appropriate pages on my website when pitching for new work and it saves time scanning and emailing cuttings.

Many independent journalists have poor websites that are lacking detail. You would not open a car dealership or kitchen showroom without all the relevant brochures. Why do the same with what is, effectively, your shop front?

Have my website and use of social media been instrumental to me earning well? The short answer is no. Have they been useful for research, for promoting myself and for keeping in touch with contacts? Undoubtedly, yes. They have made some aspects of my job easier. Twitter has kept me up to date with breaking stories in a way that no other media could.

Getting to grips with social media and learning to use it efficiently is what we all need to do, especially in an age when we all spend too much time glued to screens. Learning self-control is key.

In brief

- Keep social media in your armoury for contacting people.

- Don't use social media to procrastinate.

- Walk the dog.

- Be just as careful with what you post as you are when writing an article for a newspaper.

- There's nothing wrong with being frivolous, but if your followers are your clients be careful when you post and what you say.

- Do not post when drunk.

- Do not be a nasty loudmouth.

- Use social platforms responsibly.

- Show your best side.

- Know who your followers are.

- Social media posts can come back to haunt years later.

- Exercise self-control.

- Your website is your showroom.

Chapter 12

Interview technique: prioritise the horse's mouth over its arse

'This capacity for empathy enables a true human dialogue in which words, ideas and questions arise from an experience of fraternity and shared humanity'

Pope Francis

What you ask, how you ask it, when you ask it and where you ask it are key to ending up with a great piece of work.

Any idiot can ask questions, but asking the right questions at the right time is an art form. This requires having empathy with your interviewee, reading body language or, if on the phone, silences, hesitation, nervousness and mood. The ability to persuade people to give you true insight into themselves, a subject, other people, or an investigation is for them to trust you or to feel their only option is to answer your questions.

A journalist must adjust their interview technique for each style of interview. If you are writing a profile of a business leader, you want to get them on side as early as you can. When I first started doing business interviews, in the early part of the employed period of my career,

I would often come clean with my interviewee and tell them I was new to the subject and I was relying on their expertise and experience to talk me through it. I told them I wanted to talk to them because they were the expert. My job was to ask them the right questions and present their answers in a comprehensible way that enlightened the reader. That, for the most part, made them empathetic. They wanted to help me and it appealed to those with big egos. Perhaps they remembered when they were a rookie. It worked for the most part. As I progressed, I would feign a bit more ignorance than was the case. In that way, I was eventually able to work my way around to the killer questions that got me terrific angles or pieces of information that would not have generally been divulged to someone they perceived as a seasoned journalist of whom they should be wary. I helped my subjects warm to me.

I did everything possible to help interviewees relax into the interview. Even established chief executives can show signs of nerves when in front of a journalist. When I was more experienced, I told interviewees I was profiling that it was my wish for them to enjoy 'our chat'. I told them I was not writing an exposé for *News of the World*. I wanted to speak to them because they were a huge success and I wanted to help readers understand what had brought them to that point and, if they were willing, to share plans for the business. I would say right from the start that anything they wanted to tell me 'off the record' or that they wanted unattributed to them I would respect. At the end of the interview, I would raise those points again and see if I could persuade them to go on the record. This never failed to help them trust me.

Relaxed and friendly in face-to-face interviews was always key to getting people to drop their guard. Show humility and respect for their position without being ingratiating and creepy. If they offer you a cup of tea, accept it. All the mood music must be right. Offer something about yourself. Be 'giving' if time allows. If there is a PR person in the room don't let them stage-manage proceedings. They should be there to help and not to impede. Their function should also be to provide you with any data that your interviewee does not have to hand. All your attention should be focused on your interviewee. Treat them with care and with love and imbue them with confidence.

When interviewing on the phone for news, you still need to get your interviewee's confidence, even if they are a conman selling non-existent timeshares in some God forsaken part of the globe. Be polite but firm and do not, under any circumstances, let them avoid answering. The key is to keep them on the phone. Once they slam the phone down, you get nothing apart from a 'declined to comment'.

Should this happen, you could phone back and say you think the line went dead to continue the questioning. I did that on a couple of occasions and the subject was so flustered, I got a little bit more from them.

Tell news story interviewees you want to give them an opportunity to present their side. If they are dodgy, in the case of 'dodgy' business behaviour, say 'Look, I appreciate you are just trying to make a living,' so they think you are a bit dim and that they can manipulate you. Get their guard down, then come in with the killer questions, swoop for the kill. Do it so lovingly and innocently that they do not recognise when you have got your claws into them.

When you attend an interviewee's workplace, you can ease into the good stuff. Start with the easy questions. It might be about an award they have won or a promotion. They may have given you an hour of their time, so you have time to break them in gently before you get onto the juicy stuff. The more relaxed and confident they are with you, the more they will reveal. Go straight in with hard-core questions and they will feel you are coming on too strong and clam up.

Time is of the essence when you interview on the phone. You have caught someone in the middle of lunch, on their way to a meeting, picking the kids up from school, on their way to a romantic tryst. Just get your news questions in as fast as you can. Fire them off quickly so the interviewee does not have too much time to think about what they have just revealed. Always be courteous. Allow for silences—people hate silences. They might garble something else—the killer quote.

But silences can also be an excuse for the interviewee to say 'Right, then, if that is all, I have got a meeting.' Experienced company directors are good at that. When interviewees told me they would give me a call later, I would emphasise that deadlines dictated that I must do this now and then quickly ask as many questions as I could. It can sometimes pay to arrange a more convenient time to speak, but knowing whether someone intends to speak to you at that time or not comes with experience. You get to learn when they really mean they will speak to you at 3.30pm or whether they are fobbing you off.

During the past five years or so, I have conducted many of my interviews by email. This is efficient on time and labour. But although it is efficient, it is often not sufficient. The problem with emailed interviews is that you do not get spontaneous answers. They have time to think about what they are saying. That can be a good thing because you can often get more detail, statistics and research, but it can also enable interviewees to be manipulative and so you cannot get in quickly with a follow-up question. It can become unwieldy with emails going backwards and forward seeking clarification and asking follow-ups. Not everyone is a writer like you are. Their answers can be ambiguous.

Ambiguity is a journalist's enemy and can get you into trouble if you do not follow up to seek clarity.

Sometimes, from a legal standpoint, written answers can be helpful if you do not try to read something into them that is not there. You cannot see the person's facial expression, gauge the awkward silences, hear the hesitation and tone of voice which can give away so much. Be cognisant to the fact that a PR person might have run their eye over it or even written it. As I always say, I much prefer the horse's mouth to its arse.

During my career, I have interviewed people about highly technical subjects, including computers, internet security, online shopping, new apps, tax law and finance. If I feel out of my depth, I say that for the reader to understand what they are saying, *I* need to understand it, so please explain it to me like I'm a two-year-old. I got that one from the film, *Philadelphia*. I explain that I am not a specialist like they are, so I need them to help me with this. It works. Nothing is so complicated that it cannot be simplified. People in the computer/software industry frequently obfuscate by talking in their own tech-lingo. That is their failing, not the journalist's. Often, I found, when PR people pitched technology stories to me and they used jargon, they did not understand it themselves and had not got their clients to explain. Never feel stupid asking them to explain themselves in simple English. You must understand if you are going to make your readers understand.

Make a study of interviewees you admire, such as Jeremy Paxman, who in 1997 asked former Conservative leader Michael Howard the same question 12 times about the controversial dismissal of the head of the prison service, Derek Lewis. It was a beautiful example of exceptional interview technique and was almost painful to watch as Howard wriggled and writhed. For a completely different style, watch

Sir Michael Parkinson, who uses empathy to get his interviewees to thaw.

Successful interviewing is about the ability to wear interviewees' shoes. Empathy is everything. So is preparation. Write down all the key questions you must get in and cross them off as you go along. There is nothing worse than getting to the end of your allotted hour and finding you've not asked the most important questions. Research your interviewee. They will treat you seriously if they can see you have bothered to find out as much as you can about them. It shows you are a professional.

Interviewees, especially at director level, can seek to control the interview. Do not let them, under any circumstances. You are the interviewer and you are in control. It is *your* party. Ordinary members of the public, like animals, can be unpredictable so control is, once again, crucial.

On a final note, do not look at the clock or, at least, do not make it obvious. You should have an innate sense of the passage of time. Stifle all yawns and, if you sneeze, for God's sake do it into a tissue and say 'Excuse me!' Showering your interviewee with snot will not elicit the answers you are after.

In brief

- Prep, prep, prep.
- Write a list of questions to ensure you do not leave anything important out. Tune in to your interviewee.
- Exert your control of the interview process from the off.
- Use introductory fluff to warm up the interviewee before launching into the gold nuggets.

- If you are a novice, come clean—your interviewee was a novice once.

- Clarify ambiguities.

- If you do not understand something, say so. A professional will only be too pleased that you want to understand properly.

- Study consummate interviewers and their techniques.

- There is no time like now. If someone says they will call you back, get the most you can while they are on the phone, now.

- Ask the right questions at the right time.

- If interviewing the man or woman in the street, remember that, like animals, they are unpredictable.

- Emailed interviews require meticulous structuring and the ability to follow up.

Chapter 13

Hold your clients close and their accountants closer

'Kindness is the language the deaf can hear and the blind can see'

Mark Twain

We all like to be loved, appreciated, thought of, remembered and cherished. Our clients are no exception. Love your clients and their accountants. You might find they are human. Christmas cards are a must even if they do not reciprocate.

I often made a point of sending customers' accounts departments Christmas cards. I made sure I knew them all by name. One publishing company accountant phoned me one year and said: 'No one ever thinks of us at Christmas, thank you so much.' I have never forgotten that. When I have needed those accountants to pay me quickly or shove a payment to be signed off in front of the appropriate director they did so with alacrity. Thinking of them as more than just a faceless bean counter and ensuring I was no longer faceless to them made a huge difference.

My IT guru, as described in the chapter *Love your IT guru*, is another good example of showing appreciation for those I rely on. I send him a not unsubstantial food/drink/cheese hamper every Christmas. He always tells me there is no need, but I am so grateful to him that I want to, and I want him to understand that I am indebted to him and do not take his invaluable help for granted.

Then there are other freelance journalists that I have hired or that I simply know. It always pays to be well connected and some of them I also consider friends; not best friends but people I would enjoy a drink or a meal with. I would send them a Christmas card—even old colleagues from my employed days. It is so easy to forget that people we deal with are human, too. They have real lives with real problems, children who need clothing and feeding, elderly parents with dementia, financial difficulties.

I have always believed in treating everyone with kindness, unless they try to pull one over on me, adversely impact my livelihood, or cancel a work booking at the last moment. I remember during the '90s, one magazine editor cancelled my booking the day before, because she had got someone's holiday dates wrong. I had shuffled other work about to accommodate and the late cancellation would have meant lost income. I let her know, first politely, that she could not do that. She failed to see my point and so I made it again more forcefully. That was the last time we dealt with each other.

Many of my clients never send me Christmas cards. That rankles a bit. It would make me feel a bit more appreciated. But I have always told myself, if they kept paying me, and on time and gave me work, that was good enough. Every time they commissioned me they were saying they appreciated me, in any case, otherwise why bother using me?

As service providers, the most we can expect from our clients is timely payment. That is good enough. Anything else: friendliness, Christmas cards, commiseration on the death of the cat—they are bonuses and give us warm feelings about those we work for, but they are not germane to our ability to earn a living.

In brief

- Send clients and their accountants Christmas cards.
- Treat everyone kindly.
- Do not expect appreciation to be returned.
- Be grateful for timely payment—anything else is a bonus.

Chapter 14

Movers and groovers

'Change is never painful. Only the resistance to change is painful'

Gautama The Lord Buddha

The title of this chapter is tongue in cheek. It is the source of my worst proofreading error, which appeared in the first issue of the magazine I launched for the NHF, *SalonFocus*. The Movers and groovers column was a 'people' column—personnel moves, promotions and achievements. I failed to notice the column title had come out as 'Movers and grovers' on the final proofing. No one, as far as I am aware, noticed on publication, apart from me and the designer, Peter Greenwood, of Outhouse Creative, and publisher Eileen Lawson. I never made a mistake like that again and it has remained our secret until this day.

Like hairdressing, journalism has a lot of movers and groovers. This makes a healthy interest in people moves a lucrative part of the job. When people who commission you move to new jobs, follow them. When new people take over their previous jobs, introduce yourself to them. If you have worked for their predecessor, they are more likely to use you.

Be friendly to the junior reporter who answers the phone. One day, she might be editor. I have always been kind to people on the lower rungs, not just because there is a long-term business gain from being so but because it is the human thing to be, and we can all remember when we were the dogsbody who had to get the sandwiches and coffee for the rest of the office.

Many individuals who have commissioned me, over an independent career of thirty-odd years, have been hired and fired. Some became independents and never hacked it like I did. Sometimes the ones that could not hack it were the ones who had treated their independents badly when they were staff. What comes around goes around, so to speak.

Staff who move to new jobs present an opportunity to discover new markets. When, for example, Jenni Middleton, who rated me highly when she was editor of *Retail Jeweller*, moved to *Professional Beauty*, she gave me work on her new magazine, too. When Rachel Mackett, news editor of *Hairdressers' Journal*, moved to *Salon Business*, she commissioned me features on her new publication.

Time and time again, new markets opened to me when people moved jobs. I nurtured them and I nurtured their replacements. It is following people who move from job to job that helps the independent journalist build up a healthy portfolio of outlets.

Recommendation within publishing companies also works a treat. Journalists at many publishing groups often recommended me to their colleagues on other publications and I got work through word of mouth.

I found persistence always paid. If in 1998, a magazine said it had no extra cash to commission me, I went back to it in 2000, 2004 and 2008. Eventually I would get the gig. If I did not get a gig because of an unenlightened editor, I would wait until their replacement was *in situ*. It is like investing in the stock market: always play the long game.

An example of this was *Fine Food Digest*. I called editor Mick Whitworth numerous times trying to get regular work. He knew me of old when I wrote a column for a magazine he edited called *Fish Trader*. The final time, I was almost resigned to him repeating the same old thing, but timing is everything. I was led to believe that management wanted news shaken up a bit and Whitworth knew I was the man to do it. So began a regular news stint that lasted for several years. It was not the biggest payer, but it was regular and reliable. Alongside all my other work, it all added up to a good living, and it gave me another string to my food industry bow.

It does not matter how many times someone says no. Circumstances change, budgets change, staff leave, people get ill. Keep you name in commissioners' minds so that when opportunities arise you can grab them.

Keep an eye out for those circulars that land in your inbox that tell you who has moved where. You will discover new markets you have not thought of and editorial staff you have not previously approached. Read the likes of *Press Gazette* online, *Journalism.co.uk* and anything the NUJ puts out and get on mailing lists such as *Responsesource*, Sian Meades' *Freelance Writing Jobs*, Cision's *Media Moves, and Jobs*, and *Pitchwhiz*, and sign up to *Content Cloud* (See Chapter 21 for helpful resources).

In brief

- Be aware of how you speak to people on the way up. They might respond in kind if you are ever on the way down.

- Sign up to email circulars that tell you about personnel moves and freelance vacancies.

- Stay in touch with people who change jobs and their replacements.

- Ask clients to recommend you if they are happy with your work.

- If someone says they cannot use you at that time, contact them every six months; situations and budgets change—persistence pays!

Chapter 15

Professional snobbery means poverty

'For success, attitude is equally important as ability'

Sir Walter Scott

Never be too proud. Independents who proclaim they will only write for the quality dailies or the tabloids can quickly fall on hard times. As an independent you must ensure you are always working.

Fill in quiet patches with work you might regard as beneath you—commercial internet content, copy for ad agencies, speeches for businesspeople, articles for low-circulation magazines that pay peanuts and whose editors have as much clout as a tennis racket with broken strings.

It is always better to be working and earning something rather than biting your fingernails and getting ever more anxious as the quiet patch lingers.

Chances are you will get the great commissions again, but insulate yourself during quiet times, recessions and pandemics as best you can. We all have quiet times. Use them as opportunities to approach new markets, think up new ideas, explore how you can recycle and adapt.

A businessman who unsuccessfully sued a car manufacturer hired me once to come along with him to his solicitors to discuss ways in which we could work together. I was quite happy to accept his money even though it was far removed from mainstream journalism.

A PR company hired me to interview their clients which they then planned to use to drum up publicity. I was not too proud that I would turn it down. The Pet Care Trust hired me to write press releases for a short time when a contact who previously worked for the NHF joined. I love animals, I hate PR, but hell, if it pays my council tax, who cares? Often when you are an independent journalist you have to kiss lots of frogs before the prince or princess jobs kiss you.

Independent journalists are in the perfect space to offer their services as media trainers to corporate clients. There is lots of potential money to be earned. I never personally got involved in corporate training, but it is something any experienced independent journalist can do, because I cannot think of any company that can say they have got dealing with the media completely right for their own agenda.

For those who prefer to focus on their core skills and work, re-view previous features and news articles. Could you come up with follow-ups? Has the story moved on? While everyone else is churning out press-released stories, use this as an opportunity to pitch with original content—the ideas that make you stand out from the pack.

It never fails to astound me the number of publications that fail to routinely explore their previous issues to see if there are any stories they could move on to the next stage.

One of the hallmarks of my success, when I worked for *Super-Marketing*, was my insistence that my reporters turbo-charged their own stories by scrutinising them for the potential for new angles and developments. It is a great way to get under the skin of an issue or business, get to know it intimately and come up with exclusive news stories.

I continued to do this as an independent, because I knew few publications delved through their own archives, and it was a way I could nail stories where staff journalists thought none could be had.

Use the time to review your website and your use of social media. Call in favours to get work. When I got the call I had been dreading from *EGi's* editor, Damian Wild, in 2013 that they were giving me six months' notice, which I had had the foresight to write into my contract 17 years earlier, my stomach dropped. I had hoped this client would see me through to the life change that I have now made—albeit two years later than I had intended.

The NUJ got a solicitor to look at whether I was, in fact, technically employed by *EGi*, in which case I could have pressed for a big wad of cash, but the solicitor said it would have been nigh on impossible to argue I was employed.

I sank into a major depression and my anxiety levels rocketed. I called everyone in the industry I knew, called in favours, renewed old contacts. It was not long before my Outlook calendar was bulging with commissions.

Peter Martin hired me as managing editor of *Peach Report, Fine Food Digest*, gave me an initial ten days of work each month, *The Grocer* hired me, then *Convenience Store, The Publican's Morning Advertiser*… and many others. My basket was suddenly filled with many eggs.

I scoured the regular newsletters that regularly landed in my inbox identifying who had left where and who had joined x, y and z. There would be a pitching opportunity in each announcement.

I looked at when publications were hiring news editors or senior reporters and called those publications, knowing they were a journalist down and therefore might be able to use an independent until they hired. One such enquiry landed me with a regular three-day a week news stint for two years with *The Grocer*, another six months working twice a week for *Convenience Store*, another, working for several months every day of the week for *MCA*.

I was not proud. I had to keep the money rolling in and I did. Certainly, the last seven years leading up to my move to Wales were not as lucrative as between 1996 and 2013, but I still earned well enough to be able to fulfil my dream of changing my life while still in my fifties.

The skills journalists have can be turned to many different money-making opportunities. They are limitless.

In brief

- Pride comes before a fall.

- Be prepared to write anything for anyone.

- It is better to be working and earning than holding out for cream the cat may never get.

- Quiet times are opportunities.

- Corporate media training/consultancy could be lucrative.

- Revisit old material and ask if there are updates or linked stories you could work on and sell.

- Call in favours as and when needed.

- Keep an ear open for industry changes.

Chapter 16

Shoot the messenger

'Tricks and treachery are the practice of fools that don't have brains enough to be honest'

Benjamin Franklin

The public relations (PR)-journalist relationship has forever been a 'them-and-us' story. Most good journalists love to hate PRs like over-boiled 1970s' school cabbage.

I will try to be balanced about this, because I have dealt with many good PRs and they are invaluable, but I have found, throughout my career, that many PRs get in the way of the story. They do this by blocking access, rather than facilitating it, throwing out red herrings, failing to comprehend deadlines and returning calls and emails tardily, if at all. Many of them cannot write; they send out press releases that are ad puffs rather than news or get to the point in the penultimate paragraph. In their defence, they may say they are doing what their clients require of them, but it should be part and parcel of their role that they steer their client and not the other way around.

Their email introduction might begin: 'Fantastic news, my client's new app is in the Apple Store.' No shit Sherlock! Now go away and get back under a rock.

PRs often claim we are dishonest, cut-throat, misquote and harangue their clients, but some of them understand journalists and, instead of standing in the way of the story, help with the legwork. I have had good working relationships with some PRs who have made my job easier.

Never forget what the qualifications are for a really good story: something that someone, somewhere does not want printed or something that educates, informs and gives the reader another way of looking at a subject or issue, or something that becomes a catalyst for change—take the news coverage that inspired Sir Bob Geldof to launch Live Aid, for example, Watergate or MPs expenses.

There are too many PRs. Industry estimates suggest PRs outnumber journalists by about six to one. Journalists get hassled by PRs pitching stories that are either unworthy, or badly targeted and lacking in the information needed.

Too many of them fail to explain properly to their clients what it is that journalists need or advise them badly on managing a crisis, forgetting that the truth will always out.

Too many PRs think journalists are an extension of themselves and their remit. Wrong. We do not give a duck's fart whether their clients are happy or not with what has been reported. When a PR calls me and says: 'Our client was so delighted with your story!' I feel I have failed. Our remit is to satisfy our readers, not a PR's clients, although there are many occasions when a PR's client will feel coverage has done them justice and has been good for them.

Journalists largely feel that those who switch from journalism to PR have 'sold out' or 'gone over to the dark side'. They may feel that those people have forsaken their journalistic integrity for the lure of bigger bucks. However, it would do many of the good PRs an injustice to generalise.

I have always found PR agency personnel are the worst to deal with, many failing to think like journalists. The worst ones promise to provide information required by a deadline and then fail to deliver. I created my own PR agency blacklist so that I always gave the bad ones a wide berth the next time they came knocking. The very worst PR agencies rope in an intern to phone journalists when they are working under pressure, bleating: 'Did you get our press release?'

'Um! Which one of the thousands of rubbishy tomes that smother my inbox every day? Listen, if I got your press release and it was of any use to me and you read all the publications you are trying to target, you would know the answer.'

I have always tried not to be unreasonable with PRs—they've got a job to do—but if they behave like imbeciles, I will treat them as such.

I could write a book on my bad experiences with the PR industry, but I have also encountered those that are gold dust and worth their money and then some, and they include agency PRs. I have a lot of time for good PRs—those who have decided to promote good causes, such as charities, those who are passionate about, and believe in, the entity they are trying to promote, or those from commercial organisations that have a story to tell—especially if they have appreciated I am independent and I need the heads-up before staffers.

When I first went independent, research agency Mintel had a great in-house PR who would give me exclusive access to market reports on the basis that I could get exposure for the reports in numerous newspapers and magazines.

It was a great relationship that earned me a good deal of money by sending different versions of the same story to multiple publications. The arrangement worked for Mintel, too. I had similar relationships with several other market research houses, which, sadly, in the last decade, have become much more anal about releasing reports in their entirety, early, seemingly fearful that their clients would read so many facts and figures in the press from their reports that they would not want to pay for the full publication.

Some of the worst PRs I have encountered were in the hairdressing industry, but there were good ones, too. One stood out above everyone else for making my job a lot easier when I was editor of *SalonFocus*— Sally Learmouth, of Gloss Communications, which had an impressive roster of high-profile hairdressing industry clients.

When I was editor, I put my focus on providing strong news pages on the basis that if you have exclusive news, the rest falls into place. I would generate my own news stories, but Learmouth provided me with great business features written by experts in the industry. They were easy to edit and included all the information that I had briefed her on.

They were largely how-to type features that taught the readership something they did not know or gave them useful advice about how to run different aspects of their business better. She therefore saved me time. Time is money when you are an independent and I am grateful to her.

Another PR who was particularly helpful was Geoff Simpson, who headed the PR department at the former Co-operative Wholesale Society. He knew what journalists wanted and helped them get it. What he often gave me was unattributable but enough to enable me to stand up the stories with other sources. Most importantly, I could trust him not to withhold and not to obfuscate.

Befriend the PRs who understand your job and ignore the ones who do not. As I always say, why go to the stable boy when you can go straight to the jockey. PRs should help facilitate a story, but if they are the source, always question their motivation.

When you get a press release, pick your own angle, not the angle they are trying to push. Work to your agenda, not theirs. If you pursue an angle that their clients wanted hidden—tough! The PRs should have thought of that and had a strategy for every possible angle a journalist might take.

Always, ALWAYS ignore PRs who begin their emails with 'Hey, I just wanted to reach out to you!' Sorry, I do not want a cuddle today, or, as they say in Wales, a *cwtch*. And those who utter 'My bad!' when they make a mistake should be exterminated. 'My bad!' is not language any professional should use.

In brief

- Befriend good PRs. Ignore the rest.
- If anyone calls on deadline and asks if you got their press release, tell them where to stick it.
- Form partnerships/agreements with PRs who give you the heads-up, exclusives and understand your mindset.
- Compile a PR blacklist and create 'rules' on your email client to block them.

- Always pick your own angle from press releases and do not necessarily follow the track the PR intended.

- If anyone wants to reach out to you, hang up.

- If any PR says 'My bad!', tell them to do one.

Chapter 17

Downtime—look after yourself

'An early-morning walk is a blessing for the whole day'

Henry David Thoreau

Self-employment can be painfully lonely especially for singles. I was single for the first two years of my freedom from employment. I loved that I could make my own living—free, for the most part, from office politics. The isolation, however, was hard to manage. You need to love your own company if you live and work alone.

I found the endless hours of my own company an excruciating experience. Those who have sat with me in the pub will appreciate this. My dog, budgie, guitar and piano were lifesavers. I did not love myself much. Girlfriends had been few and far between and ten years after Sarah, the first love of my life, jilted me, I was still in mourning. Anyone else I met did not match up. Also, I had not reconciled myself with a traumatic childhood, which made rejection all the harder to accept, and the more isolated I was, the more my various neuroses came to the fore.

I engaged Dorothy, a wonderful counsellor, and subsequently another, Asaf, who I thought was more nuts than I, but we had a great chemistry that helped me move on with my life. So began many years of soul-searching during which I unpicked my childhood experiences, relationships and patterns of self-destructive behaviours.

Two years into 'therapy' with Dorothy I met Liz, a travel agent. Six weeks later we got engaged. Just like my work, when I am serious about something, I do not mess about. We have now been married 27 years.

So successful was I at unravelling my demons, I moved to what I considered to be a more enlightened state of being, and I developed skills and empathy that were innate in Liz and that led us to adopt two children. You could say loneliness and aloneness went right out the window. Somewhere along the line, I learned to love my own company—even crave it at times. You get to learn a lot about yourself when you adopt children who have had their own traumatic start to life.

Parenting, I felt, at that stage of my life, was a vocation as much as, if not more than, my day job. I am not religious, but I felt sometimes that someone or something out there was looking out for us in the first few years of adopting.

My earnings hit their all-time high and, despite my early starts, I somehow had enough energy to balance all the different parts of my life. This became harder when I developed thyroid disease, but I managed to keep all the different balls juggling aloft.

In the few weeks since I started writing this book, COVID-19 swept every other story off the front pages and independent journalists everywhere were in a state of high anxiety in common with most people who feared not only for their livelihoods but also for their health.

Those working in B2B have had an horrendous time, especially in the hospitality and travel sector—two of my markets.

A good healthy mental attitude is vital to get through such times. I freelanced my way through two recessions and there were always opportunities.

Normally, I would encourage other independents to join a gym, use a sauna and steam room, go to exercise classes and socialise wherever you can. During a pandemic when pubs, theatres, cinemas and gyms are closed, maintaining mental health becomes more solitary.

YouTube is a great source for learning new skills, teaching yourself Yoga or Pilates. Video apps facilitate virtual get-togethers. Humans are highly adaptable—one reason we have survived as a species all this time.

During your career as an independent, if it is as long as mine has been, you will encounter periods of illness and personal loss. You have no choice but to carry on. Find things you can do that enable you to temporarily switch off from whatever is going on in your life.

I bought myself a drum kit. Whenever someone infuriated me while I was trying to tie down a story or clinch a job, I would beat a drum solo and I would feel brilliant—although it did nothing to improve my hearing loss.

Take time out to play your 'psych-up' music playlist, do press ups, stick your head out the window and scream '*I'm as mad as hell and I'm not going to take it anymore!*' (*Network*). Whatever works for you. Join a choir if you can sing. If you cannot, do not! Sign up to a reading circle, take an evening class in car mechanics or shipbuilding—whatever floats your boat. I walked rescue dogs for a short period. There are so many different things you could do to put you in a different head space.

Operating as an independent journalist can be frightfully lonely, even more so when recession and/or pandemic hit. Others are in the same boat. Always tell yourself that if you have breath in your body, you have hope.

This will pass. It always does.

In brief

- Learn to love your own company, or...
- Get therapy, and...
- A partner, if that fulfils you.
- Become a juggler without losing focus.
- Adopt a good healthy mental attitude.
- Socialise.
- Exercise.
- Do whatever you need to do to let off steam.
- Indulge an interest.
- The bad stuff will pass. It always does.

Chapter 18

Devise a long-term exit plan

'Beware of missing chances otherwise it may be altogether too late one day'

Franz Liszt

You cannot keep the same pace going when you are 55 as you could when 25 no matter how well you look after your health. It makes sense, therefore, to have an exit plan.

When I left *SuperMarketing* in October 1990, I was like a human power plant. When I moved to Wales in October 2019, I was all but depleted.

Energy levels wax and wane. You will tire more easily the older you get. If you are in your 20s you might not imagine that ever happening to you. It will. Years of slumping over a keyboard will take its toll on your musculoskeletal system and, more than likely, your eyesight will take a hit, too, staring at a screen for hours on end, day after day, week after week, year after year—you get the idea?

You will become more cynical the older you get, less tolerant of fools, which we, in our trade, encounter daily, and when an editor phones you and asks you to write a 1,500-word feature on retarder provers or weighing equipment, it becomes increasingly difficult to feign enthusiasm.

If you do not have an exit plan, create one now. You might want to work until you drop, but if you do not, you need to ensure you can afford to reduce your workload when you get older.

It is easy to splurge cash when business is going well and not set some aside for later. Use the bumper years to insure yourself for leaner times and for the day when you want to reduce your workload or pack it in. What an awful situation if you are desperate to reduce work but you have not got the financial means to do so.

Humans should not have to work until they drop unless they want to. The first 30 years of my life were hell. The older I got, the more comfortable with myself I have become. I have grown into my own skin. Work helped me establish self-worth, but my work does not define me. I am who I am, regardless of what work I am, or am not, doing.

I figure I have earned leisure time in my last trimester of life, time to be selfish, time to indulge myself and those I love. I made it this far against all the odds. Why should I not be able to sit outside on the decking in the summer, gazing out to sea, with a bottle of wine on ice and a bowl of olives instead of trying to track down a company director only to be stonewalled by the company's PRs?

We have a right, at a certain point in our lives, to reap the rewards of our hard work. Decide what it is you want and plan for it as soon as you begin your self-employment. What you want might change over time. Life events, such as bereavement and divorce, can change what it is you want, but if you put the financial planning into action as soon as you can, you can flex and change as necessary.

Having an exit plan does not have to mean curling up to die or throwing yourself on the scrapheap. My exit plan included writing all those books I never had time for when I was working full-time-extra as a journalist. My plan included growing tomato plants and chilli peppers, enjoying spending more time with my wife, dog and parrot, walking for miles, stopping off at pubs, reading lots of books. I like the idea of doing a Zoology degree at some point. We plan to travel a lot: Botswana, Australasia, Peru. I want to walk the Camino de Santiago, commune with Silverbacks in Rwanda, watch flocks of wild Du Corps cockatoos in the Solomon Islands.

COVID-19 has put a temporary hold on our travel plans, but the pandemic won't last forever (as of final edits vaccinations have begun but other COVID-19 variants have manifested themselves) and, having been infected and recovered, we know we will not die from it.

The things I have described might not be your idea of a happy, fulfilling later life, but they are mine. You can write your own list and plan for the eventuality.

My plan worked down to the month I moved to Wales. I said for years that I planned to make a major change in October 2019. It is difficult to time something so precisely when a house sale and purchase is part of the equation. But on October 17th 2019 we said goodbye to our life and home of nearly 25 years and began our new adventure.

In brief

- Devise an exit plan.
- Play Scrooge when needs must.
- Use bumper years to provide for lean times and your work exit.

- Your future desires might change, but the need to fund them will not.

Chapter 19

Never buy paperclips

'There is economy only where there is efficiency'

Benjamin Disraeli

Maximisation of profit should be your key motivation. The quicker you dispatch your words, the more jobs you can potentially take on and the more money you can make.

Some people think I am tight. I think I am prudent. I am happy to spend big bucks on a beautiful work of art and I can make that purchasing decision in a heartbeat. But I will agonise about spending a couple of quid on a toilet brush, which will bring me no ascetic pleasure at all.

You have got to look like you mean it when you first go independent. You must stand out from 'freelancers' who have been forced into their current self-employment status as someone who has deliberately chosen to start a business.

I chose to be an independent businessman and my increasingly precarious position at RBI was a positive that I used to make my self-employment dream come true. Contrast that with the person who feels their hand has been forced and whose self-employment status has been determined by circumstance rather than intent.

Start like you mean it. If you work from home, your overheads will be modest, although in winter your gas/oil and electric bills will be more than you are used to paying. But you will not be paying any more for the roof over your head. Working from home does not have the same cachet as having an independent office with a Mayfair address but you would go bust within a week.

As a journalist you are fortunate. You do not have to buy 'stock' that you sell on for whatever margin you can make. What you sell comes out of thin air, as it were—words you pluck from the ether. The quicker you email your words the more jobs you can potentially take on and the more money you can make.

Ideally though, as your reputation grows, you might be able to command more money for each job and produce less volume, so that you become the Harrods of independent journalism. It might pay for you, however, to be the cash and carry of independent journalism—pile it high—sell it in bulk and cheap. Whatever works best for you and suits your way of working is the way to go—no judgment.

Let every contact you have ever made know you are starting a business. Give your business a name. If you are a big name it is reasonable just to call yourself Robert Peston or Robert Peston Media as long as you *are* Robert Peston.

I began my independent career as QFS—Quality Freelance Service. It was totally naff in retrospect and after a year I changed it to Don's Hard News. This was such a successful name change that, to this day, many people just call me Don and think it is my first name.

My stationary has a cartoonish extra-elongated Dachshund underneath the Don's Hard News logo with the strap-line—*we go to great length for hard news.* It works, it is quirky and it cost nothing. It sticks in people's minds. It is instantly recognisable. Whenever I phone accounts departments to chase up money, the accountants comment on my quirky invoices. My invoices also promote my wife's travel business, offering discounted travel to employees of the companies I write for. It works. Liz has won new business this way.

Buy yourself decent letter paper—not just general-purpose printer/copier paper. There are times, even today, when sending a letter carries weight. You know a letter is going to be read whereas an email can end up in a spam folder or is easily ignored.

When you introduce yourself to a potential new client, follow up the initial phone call with your stylish letterhead and enclose a business card. Do not get cheap, tacky business cards from the local print shop. Get a human printer to create something stylish on good quality card stock. Remember, if it is cheap and tacky your potential client will probably think your work is cheap and tacky. Always exude quality in all your contacts.

I bought a fax machine—now pretty much redundant—and a crappy printer that came with my, equally crappy, Amstrad computer, subsequently upgraded to all-singing, all-dancing top-of-the range affairs.

I have never bought paperclips—I just kept everyone else's from the days when press releases came by post. A decent high-capacity stapler and staples, box files, filing cabinets—which can largely be replaced today with scanner and computer—hole punch, box files, lever arch files and envelope files, which helped me organise whatever subject I was researching, as well as my accounts.

Will you have a room in your home that serves as your office? It is a good idea so that the rest of the house is work-free and a place where you can leave the job behind. Get the ergonomics right, with desks at the right height and enough space to be able to spread out the tools of your trade on.

Get yourself a decent voice recorder with telephone pickup. Research this carefully. I tried a couple of duds before I found the best telephone pickup for recording phone conversations with crystal clear reproduction—an Olympus TP8. Apart from investing in the most powerful and the fastest computer you can afford, an iPad and iPhone—or whatever your preferred Android or Windows devices are—one of the most important things you will ever buy for your office is your chair.

You would spend the greatest proportion of your life on your office chair if you worked the hours I worked. Do not skimp on this. It needs to have multiple adjustments so your body can be as supported as it possibly can be. Many a journalistic career has been ended by musculoskeletal issues.

I learned the hard way when, in the first decade of the new millennium, I suffered from two slipped discs in my neck which squished a nerve root. Epidurals and guided CT injections eventually sorted me out, but the pain was excruciating and working on my early-morning work was torture for the duration.

The right lighting is important. Try to work in a room that gets the best of natural light and ensure you also have blinds on the windows that you can adjust to avoid glare on your computer screen.

Two telephone lines can be useful. If you are making lots of calls and leaving messages for people to call back, the last thing you want is for a key interviewee to get the engaged tone when he or she finally deigns to return your call. At least if you have a second line, voicemail can kick in to say you are on the other line and instruct them to leave their details so you can call them back as a matter of priority as soon as you are off the other line.

The second line has become less critical with the advent of email and social media and, indeed, I finally gave up my second line at the end of 2018, because I found most people would email me to say when they would be available.

In brief

- Keep focused on profit.
- Stand out from the crowd.
- The more words you write per minute the more money you make.
- Use a memorable trading name.
- Do not forget old-fashioned letters to get noticed.
- Get a stylish letterhead and business cards that stand out.
- Use one room as your home office and do not work anywhere else in your house.
- Get the ergonomics right and do not skimp on your office chair.

Chapter 20

Avoid wideboys—sleep at night

*'You can easily judge the character of a man by how he
treats those who can do nothing for him'*

Johann Wolfgang von Goethe

I tried to claim for the cost of dog kennels once for tax purposes—just
to keep my accountant on his toes, you understand. I endeavoured to
convince him my pooch was a guard dog and therefore protected my
home office and all the equipment therein. Just because Dawn, Lara
and, most recently, Saphira rolled over and liked their tummy tickled
was irrelevant, I argued.

Some accountants might let you get away with such an outlandish
claim but not Mark, my long-suffering bean counter. Mark ensured
I slept at night. He was straight down the line and saw to it I kept
within the rules.

I kept my books/spreadsheets up to date, recorded all outputs and
inputs meticulously, retained every receipt, however small the amount,
according to the principle, if you look after the pennies the pounds
look after themselves. This principle has guided me all my life.

Mark was there to hold my hand when I had my first—and only ever—visit from an inspector of what was then Her Majesty's Customs and Excise. It was a routine visit, customary with newly-registered businesses, and it was during the first year of my VAT registration. In came the officer, dressed in pristine white blouse. In rushed my (guard) dog from the muddy garden, and exuberantly leapt upon shocked official, licked her face and covered her blouse in muddy paw prints.

I was fortunate the official was a dog lover and saw the funny side. My accountant turned the colour of asparagus.

Mark, as you will have gathered, is not a wide boy. He is one of three best friends I have known since childhood and one of three best men at my wedding.

I have only seen him lose his temper once, and it was so out of character I thought I had passed through a wormhole into a parallel universe. We were in Pizza Hut with another of my best friends, Ron, when someone accidentally jogged Mark's chair when walking past. 'Oy, arsehole!' Mark screamed. You could have heard a pin drop.

Mark was a godsend—an angel with a calculator. I liked to test him every so often, and I liked to brighten his mundane job of keeping me out of prison.

Many of my articles would include a certain amount of statistical information, working out ratios, percentages—all things mathematical at which, as I have previously said, I stunk.

Mark was always on the end of the phone to help with conundrums such as: 'If I have 3kg of genetically modified (GM) tomatoes and buy 18lb of non-GM tomatoes, how many ounces of tomato puree will I have and what will be the ratio of non-GM tomato puree to GM tomato puree?'

Wideboys also lurk in the financial services industry, especially the unregulated sector, so pick your pension adviser carefully. Remember, you want to invest for the long term. If anyone advises you to put all your hard-earned cash into Bitcoin, run a mile and call the cops.

Be a cautious or moderately cautious investor. That way, when stock market crashes occur, you will be insulated, to some extent, because your portfolio will be balanced across a wide range of asset classes, countries, funds, indices and commodities. You may not enjoy short-term heady gains, but you will also, hopefully, avoid long-term heady losses. It is long-term trends that should interest you when investing in a pension.

My financial adviser is cautious, like me, and I like him that way. He looks after my best interests and calms me down when I phone in a panic when markets plunged as they did when COVID-19 hit.

Individual assignments can sometimes cause you grief. The commissioner might have given you a loose brief and complained that the piece you produced was not what she wanted. If briefs are not clear, go back and request clarification. Do not lie awake at night stewing over whether you have interpreted the brief correctly. Some editors do not like interpretation of a brief. They like precise execution. Hence the golden rule: know your customer.

Sometimes commissioners will come back with dozens of what are apparently 'stupid' questions—especially US publications. Keep your temper and always be courteous and reply as quickly as practically possible. No question is stupid. There is a cultural and language difference between the US and the UK so be sensitive to this. What might be stupid to you may not be to them. You must adopt a different way of working for US publications—especially the corporate ones.

Copyright grabs and demands for indemnification caused me a lot of sleepless nights, because of what I considered the unreasonableness of Goliath dictating to David. There is not much you can do about such situations except make a decision and, once made, regret nothing.

I mostly liked the editors and editorial staff I had personal contact with—my beef was not with them but with their bosses who were reluctant to make changes to their standard contracts.

I had sleepless nights when I lost *EGi*, but I proved I could bounce back from that, however devastating it was to my income at that time—at least in the short term.

Sleepless nights are pointless. You do not gain anything. You do not suddenly get a eureka moment while your thoughts neurotically go round and round your head in an endless loop. You end up exhausted and a wreck. Do not give anyone the satisfaction. They do not care. You can come back from anything if you think creatively.

Self-employment as an independent journalist is a privilege, but nothing in life is plain sailing.

Avoid wideboys—sleep at night. Accept there will be periods of frustration and anxiety.

If you play the long game, as I did, you too can achieve your dream.

I will never forget the exhilarating feeling on October 17th 2019 when the removal vans turned up at our house in north London and loaded the contents of the past 24 years for the five-hour journey to West Wales. I looked at my empty office, where I had sustained my family, and knelt and kissed the worn carpet—corny but strangely emotional. 'Thank you,' I whispered. All the hard graft and all the shit Liz and I had gone through. We had finally done it. I was proud of myself. I hoped Mum was looking down at me and that she was proud, too.

I shut the office door for the last time.

I am nothing special. If I can do it, so can you.

In brief

- Do not let your dog jump up at the tax inspector.

- Keep your accounts up to date in real time.

- Pick your pension adviser carefully.

- If your briefs have holes, go back to the commissioner.

- Know your customer.

- Make allowances for cultural differences.

- Play the long game.

- Do not claim dog kennels against tax.

- Reap the rewards.

- If I can do it, so can you—honestly, I am not special.

Chapter 21

Helpful resources

The listings below are not exhaustive but are those that I have personally found helpful. You may discover others that work particularly well for you.

Books

New Oxford Style Manual (Oxford University Press).

Writer's Handbook 2021 (J Paul Dyson, firstwriter.com, JP&A Dyson).

Collins Dictionary for Writers & Editors (Martin Manser, Collins).

English for Journalists, (Wynford Hicks, Routledge).

What's Stopping You? Why Smart People Don't Always Reach Their Potential and How You Can, (Robert Kelsey, Capstone).

From Pitch to Publication (Carole Blake, Macmillan).

The Art of Punctuation, (Noah Lukeman, Oxford University Press).

The Writer's And Artists' Year Book (SJ Watson, Bloomsbury Publishing).

Practical English Usage (Michael Swan, Oxford).

Eats, Shoots & Leaves - The Zero Tolerance Approach to Punctuation (Lynne Truss, Fourth Estate, Harper Collins).

Media Law (Geoffrey Robertson QC and Andrew Nicol QC, Penguin).

McNae's Essential Law for Journalists (Mike Dodd & Mark Hanna, OUP Oxford).

The Penguin Factfinder (David Crystal, Penguin Reference Library).

Web resources

responsesource.com

cision.co.uk

journalism.co.uk

expertsources.co.uk

pressgazette.co.uk

nuj.org.uk

alcs.co.uk

muckrack.com

headlinemoney.co.uk

Freelance work sources

thecontentcloud.net

pitchwhiz.com

sianmeadeswilliams.com/freelance-writing-jobs/

@journojobuk (Twitter)

@FreelanceWJ (Twitter)

@write_jobs (Twitter)

@writejobs (Twitter)

Lightning Source UK Ltd.
Milton Keynes UK
UKHW011202140621
385487UK00003B/96

9 781999 728366